THE RETURN OF THE NATIVE

Saint George Defeated

TWAYNE'S MASTERWORK STUDIES

Robert Lecker, General Editor

THE RETURN
OF THE NATIVE

Saint George Defeated

Brian Thomas

TWAYNE PUBLISHERS
An Imprint of Simon & Schuster Macmillan
New York

Prentice Hall International
London Mexico City New Delhi Singapore Sydney Toronto

Twayne's Masterwork Studies No. 154

The Return of the Native: Saint George Defeated
Brian Thomas

Twayne Publishers
An Imprint of Simon & Schuster Macmillan
866 Third Avenue
New York, NY 10022

Library of Congress Cataloging-in-Publication Data

Thomas, Brian, 1939–
    The return of the native : Saint George defeated / Brian Thomas.
        p. cm.—(Twayne's masterwork studies ; 154)
    Includes bibliographical references and index.
    ISBN 0-8057-8073-4—ISBN 0-8057-8117-X (pbk.)
    1. Hardy, Thomas, 1840–1928. Return of the native. I. Hardy, Thomas,
1840–1928. Return of the native. II. Title. III. Series.
PR4747.T48 1995
823'.8—dc20   94-44446
                                                                              CIP

10 9 8 7 6 5 4 3 2 1 (alk. paper)
10 9 8 7 6 5 4 3 2 1 (pbk.: alk. paper)

Printed in the United States of America.

For Lola

Contents

Contents

Note on the References and Acknowledgments

All references to *The Return of the Native* are to the Penguin paperback edition, edited with an introduction and notes by George Woodcock (Harmondsworth, England: Penguin English Library, 1978). This text is a reprint of the Macmillan Wessex Edition of 1912.

I am most grateful to Helena Berg and Professor Jeff Heath for their helpful comments on Chapter 4. I would like to offer particular thanks to Greg Stephenson and Lola Boake for reading the whole manuscript and for their encouragement and support during the writing process. I would like to thank my daughter, Jean Thomas, and my parents for their unflagging support as well. Finally, I must express my profound gratitude to Michael and Jane Millgate: I owe them both so much, and without Michael this book would never have been written.

Thomas Hardy, 1891. Photograph by Barraud.
Courtesy of Frederick B. Adams.

Chronology: Thomas Hardy's Life and Works

1837	Victoria I accedes to the throne.
1840	Thomas Hardy born, at Higher Bockhampton, near Dorchester (Casterbridge), to Thomas Hardy, a self-employed stonemason, and Jemima Hand, a maid and cook.
1846	Repeal of the Corn Laws.
1847	The railway reaches Dorchester, though the country of Hardy's childhood is still largely unaffected by industrialization.
1856	Is apprenticed to John Hicks, a Dorchester architect, eventually becoming a competent architect himself, with special training in ecclesiastical design. Witnesses the hanging at Dorchester Gaol of Martha Browne, convicted of her husband's murder.
1858	From the heath near his home, witnesses another execution, that of James Seale, through the family telescope.
1859	Charles Darwin's *On the Origin of Species* and John Stuart Mill's *On Liberty* are published.
1862	Arrives in London, going to work as an assistant in the office of Arthur Blomfield, an ecclesiastical architect.
1862–1867	In London catches up with the intellectual and cultural developments of the period: haunts the National Gallery and studies various painting techniques; becomes particularly knowledgeable about the visual art of the Renaissance. Continues his classical studies, begun in Dorset under the tutelage of Horace Moule, and reads widely, not just contemporary poetry and fiction but also such authors as Ruskin, Darwin, T. H. Huxley, Comte, and Mill. Gradually loses his

belief in Christianity. Writes much poetry and becomes interested in the theater. Begins to consider pursuing a literary career.

1863–1867 Is engaged to be married to Eliza Nicholls, a lady's maid.

1867 Breaks off the engagement, returns in poor health to Dorchester, where he again becomes an assistant to John Hicks, and begins his first novel, *The Poor Man and the Lady*, the manuscript of which he will later destroy. Falls temporarily in love with Tryphena Sparks.

1868 Submits *The Poor Man and the Lady* to the London publisher Alexander Macmillan.

1870 Meets his future wife, Emma Lavinia Gifford. Submits his second novel, *Desperate Remedies* (1871), to Macmillan, who rejects it. Submits it to another publisher, William Tinsley, who agrees to publish it, partly at Hardy's own expense.

1871 *Desperate Remedies* appears, anonymously. Finishes a third novel, *Under the Greenwood Tree* (1872). A pastoral novel, its structure anticipates the seasonal organization of *The Return of the Native* (1878).

1872 Sells the copyright of *Under the Greenwood Tree* to William Tinsley for £30. Sells the serial rights to his next novel, *A Pair of Blue Eyes* (1873), to William Tinsley and abandons architecture for novel writing. Agrees to write a novel for serialization in *Cornhill* magazine (*Far from the Madding Crowd* [1874]). His old mentor and friend, Horace Moule, commits suicide at Cambridge. Walter Pater's *Studies in the Renaissance* appears.

1874 *Far from the Madding Crowd*, another pastoral novel, is a great critical and popular success. Marries Emma Gifford, and they go to live in London.

1875 A satirical novel about fashionable London life, *The Hand of Ethelberta* (1876), serialized in *Cornhill*, is much less successful than *Far from the Madding Crowd*.

1876 Begins work on *The Return of the Native* (1878), the first of his major tragic novels. He and Emma leave London and return to Dorset, first to Swanage and then to Sturminster Newton, where they remain for nearly two years.

1878 *The Return of the Native* is serialized in *Belgravia*. Hardy and Emma leave Dorset and return to London; he begins work on *The Trumpet-Major* (1880).

1880 Begins work on *A Laodicean* (1881). The first edition of *The*

	Trumpet-Major is published by Smith, Elder. Hardy suffers a severe and lengthy illness.
1881	Becomes interested in Auguste Comte's positivism but finds it difficult to accommodate his own view of the radical imperfection of the universe with Comte's philosophy.
1882	Returns with Emma to Dorset, and they look for a plot of building land. *Two on a Tower* appears.
1883	Hardy and Emma begin building their future house, Max Gate, near Dorchester, to Hardy's own design. His reputation as a novelist is now firmly established.
1884	Begins work on *The Mayor of Casterbridge* (1886), the second of his great tragic novels. He continues to read widely, including such authors as Arnold, Carlyle, Comte, Macaulay, Mill, Stephen, Spencer, Caro, and G. H. Lewes. Also increasingly immerses himself in Dorset history.
1885	Hardy and Emma move into Max Gate.
1886	Hardy begins writing *The Woodlanders* (1887). Emma has been actively assisting him in his work for some time, though there is no evidence of actual literary creation on her part. Domestic and marital difficulties between them begin to make themselves felt.
1887	Hardy and Emma visit Italy. *The Woodlanders* appears and becomes Hardy's greatest critical success since *Far from the Madding Crowd*. Hardy begins work on *Tess of the d'Urbervilles* (1891), his third major tragic novel.
1888	Publishes *Wessex Tales,* his first collection of short stories.
1889	Publishing firm of Tillotson and Son rejects the first half of the manuscript of *Tess* on grounds of bad taste. Hardy meets similar objections from other publishers; he makes revisions.
1890	Completes *Tess*, a bowdlerized version of which is serialized in the *Graphic*.
1891	Osgood, McIlvaine publishes *Tess* in volume form, with most of the offending passages restored. Hardy publishes his second volume of short stories, *A Group of Noble Dames*. Is elected to the Athenaeum as a person of "distinguished merit" in the field of literature. Reads Schopenhauer's *Studies in Pessimism*.
1892	*The Pursuit of the Well-Beloved* appears in serial form. Begins writing *Jude the Obscure*, his final major tragic novel.
1893	Becomes deeply attracted to Florence Henniker, daughter of Richard Monckton Milnes.

1894	Publishes *Life's Little Ironies,* his third collection of short stories. Hardy and Emma are growing estranged.
1895	Publishes *Jude the Obscure.* Hostile reviews contribute to his decision to abandon writing fiction in favor of poetry.
1897	*The Well-Beloved* appears, much revised in volume form.
1898	Publishes *Wessex Poems,* his first volume of poetry. Hardy and Emma become increasingly estranged, partly because of her disapproval of his pessimism and lack of religious faith.
1899–1902	The British war against the Boers. Hardy is fascinated by the sense of historical upheaval, but has little sympathy with jingoism and imperialism.
1901	Queen Victoria dies. Hardy publishes *Poems of the Past and the Present.*
1904	Publishes the first part of *The Dynasts,* a long dramatic poem based on the Napoleonic Wars, with the second and third parts published in 1906 and 1908, respectively.
1905	Meets Florence Dugdale, and they begin a correspondence that leads to a close relationship.
1909	Publishes his third volume of poems, *Time's Laughingstocks.*
1910	Receives the Order of Merit.
1912	Macmillan publishes the Wessex Edition of Hardy's novels and poems. He receives the gold medal of the Royal Society of Literature. Emma Hardy dies, after a period of mental decline.
1913	Publishes *A Changed Man,* his fourth volume of short stories. Proposes to Florence Dugdale.
1914	Marries Florence Dugdale. World War I begins; Hardy is horrified by this, and his pessimism deepens. Publishes another volume of poetry, *Satires of Circumstance.*
1917	Increasingly horrified by the war, Hardy nevertheless maintains a high level of literary productivity. Publishes *Moments of Vision,* his fifth volume of poems. Begins work, with Florence's help, on an autobiography, later published as *The Early Years of Thomas Hardy* (1928) and *The Later Years of Thomas Hardy* (1930), disguised as a biography written by Florence.
1920	The Hardy Players, of Dorchester, present a dramatized version of *The Return of the Native.* Hardy has little to do with the adaptation but is delighted with the production, especially by the actress playing Eustacia Vye.

Chronology

1922	Publishes *Late Lyrics and Earlier*, another volume of poetry, with a particularly gloomy and bitter preface.
1923–1924	Hardy's play, *The Queen of Cornwall*, is produced.
1924–1925	Writes a dramatization of *Tess of the d'Urbervilles* for the Hardy Players and is closely involved with its production in Dorchester and London.
1925	Publishes his seventh volume of poems, *Human Shows Far Phantasies Songs and Trifles*.
1928	Dies on 11 January. His last volume of poetry, *Winter Words*, is published posthumously.

LITERARY AND
HISTORICAL CONTEXT

1

Hardy's Pessimism and the Mid-Victorian Age

Thomas Hardy was acutely sensitive to the intellectual and cultural ethos of his time, a sensitivity that derived in part from the fact that he was to a considerable extent self-educated and keenly aware of having risen above the social class into which he had been born. Although *The Return of the Native* has something of the timeless quality peculiar to all great works of art, this novel is also very much a product of the historical period in which it was written. At first glance, of course, the idea of Hardy as a novelist characteristic of his age seems slightly odd. Compared to Dickens, George Eliot, Thackeray, or Trollope, with their energetic attentiveness to the crowded and gregarious social texture of Victorian life, Hardy looks like an anomaly. He is primarily interested in remote and lonely places, in people who are essentially solitary—outsiders even. The world he evokes is typified more by a sense of gloomy ennui than by the kind of energy and optimism that we think of as Victorian.

We still tend to conceive of the Victorian era as culturally monolithic: it is, so the stereotype goes, the great age of industrialization, imperial expansion, and an almost boundless national confidence—its twin guiding stars being the idea of progress and an ideal of religious piety that now seems to verge on the fanatical. In fact, however, it was also a profoundly schismatic age, an era marked by fierce dissent in relation to nearly every kind of prevailing cultural orthodoxy. An intense debate about religious faith, to take the most obvious and dramatic example, raged almost continuously throughout the nineteenth century, and while those who came down on the side of doubt were an embattled minority, their voice was formidable and their arguments increasingly compelling. One of the most striking features of *The Return of the Native* is the way in which, indirectly but unmistakably, the novel reflects the terms and tone of that debate.

Hardy belonged among the doubters. Though he always retained a nostalgic emotional loyalty to the Anglicanism in which he had been raised in rural Dorset, he gradually lost his faith during his London years as an architect's assistant in the 1860s. By the time he began to write *The Return of the Native* in 1876, he was an agnostic. It is not just that God is absent from the novel but that this absence is conspicuous and pervasive, constituting a kind of negative organizing principle that has a profound impact on characterization, plot, and even setting. Neither Clym Yeobright nor Eustacia Vye is in any real sense a Christian believer. Although Clym becomes, nominally, a "preacher" at the end of the story, his message is humanistic rather than religious, echoing something of the positivism—the so-called religion of humanity—of Auguste Comte and something of John Stuart Mill's utilitarianism. More fundamentally, Clym represents a strain of puritanical stoicism, seeing himself as an educator whose mission is "to buckle to and teach [people] how to breast the misery they are born to."[1] Eustacia, on the other hand, is a hedonist; she is associated explicitly with the paganism of classical antiquity. When she does from time to time invoke a higher power, it is only to rail against an indeterminate but invariably hostile "Prince of the world, who had framed her situation and ruled her lot" (361). Even the heath-folk, we are told, are more pagan than Christian.

The novel's plot similarly involves a sequence of cause-and-effect that is anything but providential. Fatalism is both the prevalent mood and the governing principle on Egdon Heath: things happen as they do less by design than according to chance, accident, or coincidence, and they usually turn out badly. The only evidence of design is exhibited by the order of nature, but nature is definitively characterized by the sense of its otherness, its indifference or resistance to human aspiration. The mysterious cosmos beyond it seems also, at best, indifferent to suffering humanity and sometimes positively malevolent. Hardy had not apparently read Schopenhauer when he wrote this novel, and so he had not yet borrowed the vaguely sinister notion of a cosmic "immanent will," but such an idea is already implicit in the brooding otherness of the heath itself. Egdon, with its rare and sometimes virtually archaic forms of life, its vestiges of extinct species, is very much a Darwinian landscape. And it is of course with Darwin—or at any rate with Darwinism—that so much of Victorian agnosticism and atheism originates.

In *On the Origin of Species* (1859), which challenged the idea that the basic forms of nature were fixed and immutable, Charles Darwin argued that species either evolve or become extinct according to their relative ability to adapt to changes in the natural environment. Among other things, this theory saw humanity as having evolved from the higher animal primates, and thus it constituted a direct threat to the validity of the biblical account of Creation. It was generally regarded by Victorian Christianity as an implicitly blasphemous denial of the existence of God. But even among the Darwinists, the issue was not quite as simple as that.

Evolution could be seen as a blind, almost mechanical process, exhibiting no particular moral purpose or directedness beyond that of the survival instinct; or it could be seen as a dynamic that validated both the ideal of progress and the fundamental tenets of religious faith itself. The gradual progression from lower to higher forms of natural life might be viewed as evidence of a divine plan, and the emergence of civilized humanity as one of the stages nearer the end than the beginning of a "creative" cosmic process. This latter was the view underlying such movements as positivism, meliorism, and utilitarianism in the nineteenth century, as represented by thinkers like Comte, Spencer, and Mill. Hardy tried for a long time to accommodate the meliorist position to his own worldview, but in the end he rejected even the long-range optimism offered by the "creative" evolutionists.

For Hardy, only pessimism made sense in the context of this kind of debate. Whatever evolution might mean, it seemed clear to him that humanity had no special significance in any process dominated by the blind urges of nature and none whatever in any putative cosmic scheme of things. He saw the human condition as essentially determined by factors beyond our control. Such determinism deprives humanity, of course, of dignity and freedom, even at times making people victims of a sort of random cosmic malignity. And it is in reaction to this sense of deprivation and victimization that the Promethean note of revolt—in *The Return* represented primarily by Eustacia Vye—is sounded.

The Promethean strain also represents a continuation of the romantic theme of rebellion against the conception of a tyrannical and vengeful God—a theme that had begun to appear in English literature around the beginning of the nineteenth century, especially in poets like Blake and Shelley. For Hardy, however, even God had disappeared; all that was left was the idea of "Fate"—suffering humanity's attempt to project the embodiment of some kind of controlling force behind its perception of an amoral and purposeless universe. Whereas romantic determinism could at least allow man to see his suffering as noble and tragic, fatalism, however, diminishes him by making him altogether powerless and helpless. The sense of tragedy in Hardy's fiction always gives way, finally, to that of irony. Mrs Yeobright's death in the novel, for instance, is more ironic than tragic, and although Clym seems to be trying in the end to see himself as a heroically tragic figure, the real irony of his role and his situation is all too clear to the reader.

The pessimists in the debate over Darwinism tended to regard almost all the evidence of evolutionary change as ominous and sinister. Egdon Heath is not only a Darwinian terrain for Hardy; in imaginative terms it is primarily a monstrous place. The sense that we get of it as atavistic sometimes extends to the psychic life of its inhabitants as well. The customs and superstitions of the heath-folk tend to be vestiges of primitive modes of thought and of ancestral pagan practices. There is the animism or "fetishism" implicit, for example, in Christian Cantle's awe of the dice and in Susan Nunsuch's faith in the sympathetic magic that she tries to work against Eustacia.[2] Sympathetic magic suggests, of course, a kind of unity of humanity and nature, but the only such unity unequivocally endorsed in the novel is that of mutual suffering—as in the scenes in which the wind is described as wailing in pain on the heath or in the "Devil's Bellows."

Even more fundamentally sinister, though, is the way the novel reflects the fear implicit in Darwinism that modern civilization, far from representing a stage of evolutionary advancement, might actually constitute a phase of morbid hyperrefinement and sterility, signalling the beginning of the process of extinction. The characterization of Clym, for instance, may have been influenced by contemporary theories of a "higher" degeneracy: Clym's features "already showed that thought is a disease of flesh" (194), and they reflect the type of melancholy and spiritual exhaustion that "must enter so thoroughly into the constitution of the advanced races" (225). In a sense, both Clym and Eustacia, with their highly developed and cultivated sensibilities, can be seen as having failed—and the more stolid Diggory and Thomasin as having succeeded—in an elemental struggle of adaptation.

In this connection it is significant that the relationship between spirit and flesh in Hardy's portrait of Clym amounts to a grim parody of that which characterizes Walter Pater's accounts of the great Renaissance paintings in his *Studies in the Renaissance* (1873). Always much interested in the visual arts—his architectural background was closely related to this interest—Hardy is an intensely pictorial novelist; and Pater, one of the leading proponents of Victorian aestheticism, had an enormous influence on *The Return of the Native*. This was in the first place stylistic: the famous "Queen of Night" chapter, for example, echoes and may even be modeled on Pater's description of the enigmatically smiling lady in *La Gioconda*. But Pater had almost as great an impact on Hardy's impressionistic techniques of visualization. For Pater, the essential characteristic of the human figures in Renaissance art is that they convey mind somehow working on body, so that a sensuous outer beauty always seems to be the product of a more elusive inner spiritual quality. With the picture of Clym, however, Hardy reveals his own evolutionary outlook in regarding thought as a "parasite" (194), a disease of flesh "preying upon an outer symmetry" (194).

This is not to deny the importance, though, of Victorian aestheticism in the novel. In *Culture and Anarchy* (1869) Matthew Arnold saw the two fundamental and mutually antagonistic forces in British culture as what he called "Hellenism," the intellectual and aesthetic principle in human life, and "Hebraism," the moral principle. For Arnold, Hebraism had become too much the dominant force, and in his advocacy of Hellenism he urged a kind of national renewal of the aesthetic approach to life. From one point of view, Clym and Eustacia can be seen as the respective embodiments of these two forces, the puritanical and moralistic Clym being predominantly a Hebraic type and Eustacia his Hellenistic antitype. The hedonistic Eustacia is of course explicitly linked to the ancient Greek world; more important, her outlook and aspirations are not only Promethean but Dionysian. So the conflict between the two characters can be seen as that between the aspiring ethical life and the aspiring aesthetic one.

At the same time, Arnold's basic distinction illuminates Clym's self-division: his sense of mission may be Hebraic, but his scheme of educating and improving the cultural life of the inhabitants of Egdon, however misguided it might be, is also a Hellenistic project, one that involves the promulgation of what Arnold called "sweetness and light." So on the one hand, Clym exemplifies the distrust of aestheticism articulated in John Ruskin's view of the primacy of morality, even in art; on the other, he cannot help but be drawn to the sheer gorgeousness of Eustacia, to her spiritedness and sexuality.

Ruskin, together with Carlyle, may well have contributed something, too, to the whole idea behind Clym's decision to abandon a cosmopolitan career and to become a schoolmaster and later a cutter of furze, or gorse, which he would sell as firewood. His decision in fact reflects a more general Victorian tendency to idealize such notions as the return to the simple life and the dignity of labor. This strain of thought can be traced back to the founder of French socialism, Saint-Simon, who was not only a formative influence on Comte's positivism but is also a likely candidate as the original source of those "ethical systems popular at the time" (230) in Paris, which, we are told, impelled Clym to change his life and to return to Wessex in the first place.

Many other contemporary influences can be detected in the novel as well. There is, for example, the emphasis in Victorian education on classical studies: Arnold's "sweetness and light" refers chiefly to an ideal of rediscovering and renewing the culture of classical Greece and Rome. Partly because of his relatively humble social origins, Hardy had a particular respect for classical learning, and as a boy and a young man he labored long and hard, first under the tutelage of his early mentor, Horace Moule, and then alone, to acquire a degree of mastery in it. One result was his fascination with Greek tragedy: *The Return of the Native* was actually conceived in terms of the aesthetic principles underlying that form of drama which, with its assumptions about the centrality of the role of fate in human affairs, has certain affinities with the Darwinian cast of Hardy's thinking. Another was his interest in classical mythology. The range of the allusiveness to classical myth and legend in his fiction is immense, and this kind of referentiality tends to be integral to the structure of each of the novels—as it certainly is in *The Return*—rather than a matter simply of fancy peripheral embellishment. As we shall see, Hardy's use of mythic reference and echo demonstrates something much more basic and important about his habit of mind than a mere inclination to show off his learning. It demonstrates a habit of his imagination that is in fact arguably more significant than his engagement with any of the ideas or theories debated so hotly in his time.

2

The Importance of the Work

As the first of Hardy's great tragic novels, *The Return of the Native* is important in the first place because it represents a significant advance in his own development as a novelist. *Far from the Madding Crowd* had already marked his emergence from a literary apprenticeship in which he had experimented with various genres of fiction with varying degrees of success. But if *Far from the Madding Crowd* exhibited a new assurance with respect to both narrative texture and structure, the sense of Hardy's growing control of his materials and technique, it also reflected a continuing uncertainty about genre. The basic shape of that novel is comic, but there are powerful tragic elements in it that constantly threaten to dissolve the overall comic design; at the end the heroine seems almost diminished rather than fulfilled by her marriage to the hero. In some ways that heroine, with her independence and strength of will as well as her beauty, prefigures Eustacia Vye; but of course Eustacia is in no sense diminished at the end of *The Return of the Native,* even by her death. While Hardy retained in *The Return* the important pastoral element from *Far from the Madding Crowd,* he allowed his imaginative inclination toward tragedy a free rein. "Tragedy" is a slightly misleading term, as we shall see, for Hardy's kind of fiction; still, it is certainly true that *The Return,* with its stark vision of lonely human aspiration and pain in a natural setting perceived neither sentimentally nor merely as a backdrop for the characters, establishes a significant pattern for such subsequent texts as *Tess of the d'Urbervilles* and *Jude the Obscure.*

The novel's importance is even more considerable, however, in the larger historical context of the development of the novel as a literary form. The Victorian era may seem to us now to be the great age of the novel, but even as recently as in the latter half of the nineteenth century in Britain, its artistic reputation was relatively low. When it was not seen as merely the dominant medium of popular romance, its virtues were regarded as having to do almost solely with its social significance. There was not much interest in form. This had something to do with the commercial exigencies of serial publication and the three-volume format of most first editions, so that Henry James could refer to some of the novels of the period as "loose, baggy monsters." Sheer length was not the only problem in this respect, however: formal considerations were, even for such novelists as Dickens, Thackeray, and George Eliot, less compelling than they were to become for novelists 60 or 70 years later.

Hardy's own eventual abandonment of novel writing in favor of poetry is evidence of the fact that poetry was taken more seriously, yet one of his own achievements was to give the novel a new kind of formal integrity. *The Return of the Native*—with its unity of time and setting, its careful patterning of visual motifs and almost choreographic groupings of characters, its skillful use of repetition and variation in both its large, emblematic or iconographic episodes and its smaller, detailed scenes—established new standards of craftsmanship as well as of art.

Hardy and Henry James, although they took very different approaches and did not exhibit much in the way of mutual admiration, can be seen as the two founding fathers of the modern novel. Perhaps the most crucial formal preoccupation common to both writers was a concern with narrative perspective. Although Hardy's fiction lacks anything quite like James's sophisticated "center of consciousness" and its handling of point of view in James's sense is sometimes clumsy, perspective was nevertheless of the first importance for Hardy. *The Return* is virtually constructed around the subtle alternation of different angles of vision. People and things are constantly being seen, almost cinematically, from different visual distances, and are thereby revealed in new ways or with new kinds of significance. There is, for instance, the contrast between the magnified or "microscopic" effect of Clym's furze-cutting, as seen by himself, and the way he is reduced to nothing more than a brown speck in the landscape by Mrs. Yeobright's distant glimpse of him; or, conversely, there is the parallel between the remote view of a diminished Mrs. Yeobright struggling painfully across the vast expanse of heath and her own vision, in an abrupt shift of perspective at the moment of her collapse, of a small colony of ants just beneath her eyes. Hardy is forever expanding and contracting distances in this way in the novel, so that the great emblematic episodes, like the night gambling scene on the heath, depend for their significance not just on visual intensity but on the different kinds of meaning suggested by variations in visual perspective itself. Hardy's is by no means the sort of "unconscious" genius that critics used to assume it to be; on the contrary, as we shall see, his narratives tend to be unified on the basis of carefully constructed antithetical polarities, not only of perspective but of metaphor as well.

Besides anticipating to some extent the modernist obsession with form, Hardy also anticipates various twentieth-century themes. His portrayal of women, for example, as strong and sometimes heroically independent was close to revolutionary in Victorian fiction. It made him a peculiarly important novelist for writers like Virginia Woolf and D. H. Lawrence. For Lawrence, the intensely erotic dimension of Hardy's novels had an additionally significant resonance, and Hardy's acute psychological perceptions about both family relationships and those between men and women had an enormous influence on Lawrence's writing: *Sons and Lovers* clearly owes much to the central Clym–Mrs. Yeobright–Eustacia triangle in *The Return of the Native*. Similarly, the self-contained world of "Wessex" prefigures Faulkner's Yoknapatawpha. Hardy's preoccupation with human isolation, powerlessness, and alienation also anticipates the worlds of romantic ironists like Conrad and, later, of unromantic ironists like Beckett. The twentieth-century motif of the outsider is already clearly evident in his fiction: his imaginative sympathies tend to lie with characters at the lower end of the social scale and especially with those who find themselves in a kind of limbo somewhere between the working and middle classes, as well as with women. His apprehension of female sexuality—Eustacia Vye is a highly eroticized figure—makes Hardy seem no less "modern" than does his vision of his male heroes as in one way or another deracinated or displaced.

Quite apart from all this, however, *The Return of the Native* is important simply in itself. It is less easy to say why, but the novel's unique power seems to have something to do with what might be called its operatic quality. Although Egdon Heath is conceived in naturalistic terms, its sheer archaic strangeness also has the effect of freeing the social world of the story from the narrower confines of realistic plausibility. So the sense of passion and pathos we find there, while often melodramatic and sometimes verging on the absurd, is always on the grand scale. Hardy manages to get in touch in this novel with feelings and themes that can best be described as elemental: from our first view of Eustacia keening wordlessly on the summit of Rainbarrow to that of Mrs. Yeobright collapsing on the arid heath, and the scenes of violent anguish occasioned by that collapse, the evocation is of an intensity of human need, love, pain, and grief that seems somehow larger than life. The proposition that Hardy's gift should be regarded as unconscious was always a dubious one, but he does succeed, sometimes clumsily, in invoking potent forces that we recognize as much on the basis of our experience of dream as of reality.

Human desire and fear are characterized in *The Return of the Native* by a peculiar compulsiveness. Indeed, they have something of the hypnotic and ritualized quality that we associate with the psychological dynamics of the repetition compulsion. In the last analysis, the strength of this novel derives from the fact that Hardy deals in archetypes, and that he does so without sacrificing much in the way of realistic specificity. These are not the rather arbitrarily devised archetypes of the Jungian "collective unconscious" but the great central organizing symbols of the human imagination. The heath itself is such a symbol, having more in common with the terrain in the final scenes of

Shakespeare's *King Lear* than with any topographical reality. And the archetypal dimension of *The Return* has to do with the novel's consciously evoked mythic resonance—all the biblical and classical echoes and allusions that inform its structure.

Hardy's recognition of the informing power of myth is exactly what makes him a mythopoeic novelist. His classical and biblical references are not adornments of a theme; cumulatively, they *are* the theme. The seasonal symbolism on which the time scheme of *The Return* is based organizes the action in relation to an ongoing natural rhythm of death and rebirth, a rhythm perceived as an endless and mysterious process of sinking into and emerging out of a Hadean night world. Desire and fear are operatically compulsive in this novel precisely because they resonate endlessly in the context of what might be thought of as a primal repetition compulsion of a much larger and stranger kind—one that both shapes those human emotions and is oblivious of them.

3

Critical Reception

Until fairly recently, the critical response to Hardy's fiction could be categorized according to three main types of approach. There has been the kind of criticism that has focused on rural "Wessex" and taken its cue from a certain view of nineteenth-century history, interpreting the novels in terms of a perceived tension between an older agricultural way of life that was already vanishing by the time of Hardy's birth and the advance of industrial modernity. Then there is the approach that has concerned itself with Hardy's ideas and with the philosophical sources of those ideas, concentrating on the "metaphysics" of his fictional world. In the third place there is what has emerged as the central tradition of formalist criticism: based on the assumption of the total coherence of all the novels, this approach has been concerned to demonstrate the principles of structural unity in each case, showing how such various elements as plot, setting, characterization, narrative voice, and imagery contribute to that unity. None of these approaches is entirely discrete, of course, for there is often some overlapping among them, but each is distinct enough to be recognizable and even familiar.

To these, however, a fourth approach must now be added, one that began to gather momentum in the 1970s and that, it can be argued, currently dominates the scholarly debate. This is a criticism that rejects the assumption of coherence in the novels and examines Hardy in the light of perceived incongruities and dissonances in his fiction; like formalist criticism, it involves a close analysis of each of the texts, but it is interested primarily in subtexts and in the ways in which those subtexts tend to work against or even to undermine whatever seems to be going on at the narrative surface.[3]

The basis of each of these four critical traditions can be discerned in the earliest commentaries. Most of the contemporary reviews of *The Return of the Native* expressed disappointment and puzzlement over the novel, comparing it unfavorably with the immensely successful *Far from the Madding Crowd;* despite the reviewers' other misgivings, however, a fascination with the whole idea of "Wessex," for example, is evident from the outset in their acknowledgments of Hardy's keen observation of nature. For all its strangeness, Egdon Heath clearly belongs to a unique fictional region, and in 1889 J. M. Barrie wrote an article in the *Contemporary Review* stressing Hardy's importance as a regional and pastoral novelist. Establishing him as the "historian of Wessex," Barrie also established the critical view that sees Hardy's main concern as the vanishing of the rural way of life. In a study published in 1936 but written in 1914, D. H. Lawrence also attributed Hardy's greatness to his sense of his characters' connection with the earth, a rootedness that he understood as enabling them to live by passion and sensuality rather than by reason or convention. For Lawrence, Egdon represents raw animal instinct, an energy that he sees as magnificently embodied in Eustacia and repressed in Clym.

T. S. Eliot might have been expected, given his ideal of culture as something local, rural, and organic, to endorse some version of this view; but Eliot disliked Hardy's agnosticism, and he found a "diabolic" element in Hardy's fiction, which he saw as constituting a dead end for the development of the novel. F. R. Leavis followed Eliot's lead in this respect, excluding Hardy from his idea of "the great tradition" of English fiction on the grounds that he lacked certainty of moral purpose. Katherine Anne Porter, on the other hand, rejected the narrowness of Eliot's reading of Hardy and wrote a persuasive defense of Hardy's morality within the context of the centrality of the world of nature in his work.

The historian-of-Wessex approach was to some extent echoed as well by Virginia Woolf, who also noted the centrality of Egdon Heath in *The Return*. Because of what she saw as his very tendency, however, to lament the disappearance of the rural past, Hardy was relegated by Woolf to the status of Victorian (as opposed to modernist) writer. But Hardy's importance as a regional novelist was further endorsed by the publication of Ruth Firor's *Folkways in Thomas Hardy* in 1931 and Donald Davidson's influential essay in 1940, which presented Hardy as a kind of folkloric bard of Wessex, a writer very much rooted in a rustic and oral ballad tradition. At its worst, this critical approach descends to sentimentality, but there can be little doubt that it has always come closest to reflecting Hardy's popularity with most readers. It is an approach that was perhaps given its most sophisticated formulation by John Holloway in 1959. Holloway stressed the vitality of rural life in *The Return* and contrasted it with the novel's treatment of the sterility of modernity: he saw the story as constructed around a basic clash between, on the one hand, Clym, Wildeve, and Eustacia as representatives of a modern and essentially urban alienation and, on the other, Diggory and Thomasin as representatives of the virtues of the old agricultural order. This kind of view, also advanced by such critics as Douglas Brown and Arnold Kettle, has gradually become much less influential.

The influence of the school of thought that has been concerned to explicate Hardy's "philosophy" has also waned in the last 20 years or so. Hardy's interest in ideas is evident in nearly all his novels, but from the outset his ideas have been regarded as problematic. Critics have tended to find them unpalatable, inconsistent, or obtrusive. The earliest reviewers of *The Return of the Native* complained not only about "gloom" and "pessimism" but also about Hardy's habit of rather ponderous metaphysical theorizing. His ideas were seen as having the effect of disfiguring his story, and one of the earliest critical themes was that of the conflict between Hardy's intellect and his imagination. In the *New Quarterly Magazine* of October 1879, for example, the reviewer regards *The Return* as having failed to fulfill the promise of the earlier novels and sees its philosophical dimension as especially ominous; regarding Hardy's future career this reviewer asks, "Will the unconscious inspiration assimilate the [philosophical] motive? or will the consciousness of the motive paralyse the inspiration?" The question is the genesis of the notion, later amplified by Virginia Woolf, that Hardy's artistry somehow had little to do with the workings of his conscious mind. Despite this view, however, there has been no shortage of book-length studies of Hardy's philosophy, from Helen Garwood's *Thomas Hardy: An Illustration of the Philosophy of Schopenhauer* (1911) to G. W. Sherman's *The Pessimism of Thomas Hardy* (1976). Other prominent analysts of Hardy's ideas include Herbert Grimsditch, Ernest Brennecke, Patrick Braybrooke, A. P. Elliott, and F. R. Southerington.

Following the example of D. H. Lawrence, many critics have simply dismissed or ignored the element of metaphysics in Hardy's fiction. For Lawrence, as for Woolf, Hardy is truest to himself in *The Return* when he forgets about philosophy and turns to the sensuous evocation of Egdon itself. Others, like John Holloway, have argued that the ideas are in fact assimilated by the imaginative vision; Roy Morrell goes further by maintaining that the bleakness of the philosophy is actually considerably modified in this process of imaginative absorption. For the most part, though, Hardy's "thought" has been regarded as extraneous: by the time of the ascendancy of the New Criticism in the 1950s and 1960s, critics like Albert J. Guerard echoed F. R. Leavis's dislike of Hardy's narratorial philosophizing, but on aesthetic rather than moral grounds. In its demonstration of Hardy's thoroughgoing professionalism, Michael Millgate's *Thomas Hardy: His Career as a Novelist* (1971) disposed conclusively of the idea of a split between the laborious "thinker" and the "unconscious" artist, thus perhaps clearing the way for a reconsideration of the novels' philosophical elements. Jean R. Brooks's *Thomas Hardy: The Poetic Structure,* also published in 1971, argued that Hardy's ideas can be seen as constituting an anticipation of mid-twentieth-century existentialism and absurdism. Since then, however, not much that is new or of great interest has emerged on the subject.

The formalist approach to Hardy, with its assumption of coherence and unity in the novels, has been the dominant one. The aesthetic form of *The Return of the Native* has been analyzed in various contexts and perspectives—dramatic, psychoanalytic, pictorial, and mythic, to name only a few. The first book-length study, Lionel Johnson's *The Art of Thomas Hardy* (1894), saw *The Return* as Hardy's best novel, largely because of the principles of formal economy on which the story is constructed. The relevance of Hardy's pictorial technique to the novel's structure was first noted in Annie Macdonell's *Thomas Hardy,* also published in 1894. Whereas in *Thomas Hardy: A Critical Study* (1912) Lascelles Abercrombie regarded the form of *The Return* as dramatic, Harold Child's *Thomas Hardy* (1916) picked up Macdonell's theme by concentrating on the novel's visual element, though he also agreed with Abercrombie's evaluation of *The Return* as one of Hardy's four great novels of "dramatic form." Child's argument is centered on optics and angles of vision, and in this respect his study looks forward to ideas explored by Joseph Warren Beach and, later, David Lodge and others, about the ways in which Hardy seemed to anticipate cinematic techniques. In 1921 Samuel Chew's *Thomas Hardy: Poet and Novelist* issued a veiled challenge to Henry James's assessment of the carelessness of Hardy's craftsmanship by arguing that Hardy had his own distinctive "theory" of the novel and that this is implicit in his fiction.

Joseph Warren Beach's *The Technique of Thomas Hardy* (1922) is generally regarded as the first important formalist study. Beach attended exclusively to issues pertaining to technique and structure in the novels, and he elaborated the earlier ideas about both dramatic and pictorial form in a highly sophisticated way. His reading of *The Return of the Native* as a kind of fictional equivalent of classical tragedy has been enormously influential, especially in relation to later studies of tragic form in Hardy's writing, like Dale Kramer's in 1975. In 1927 Mary Ellen Chase published *Thomas Hardy: From Serial to Novel,* a work that made much illuminating use of Beach's approach. In some ways Beach can also be regarded as the forerunner of the formalism of the New Critics, whose foray into Hardy territory came in the Hardy centennial number of the *Southern Review* in 1940. With this influential publication, contributors like Arthur Mizener, Allen Tate, Donald Davidson, and Morton Dauwen Zabel established a new standard of excellence in Hardy criticism. Several of the articles from the 1940 *Southern Review* were reprinted in the equally authoritative *Hardy* of 1963, edited by Albert J. Guerard. Interestingly, Guerard's own monograph, *Thomas Hardy* (1949), objected to the high place accorded *The Return* by Abercrombie and Beach precisely on the basis of what he saw as Hardy's excessive preoccupation with form in that novel. Guerard may well have been reacting to some of the more intricately ingenious New Critical readings of *The Return*, like R. W. Stallman's "Hardy's Hour-Glass Novel" (1947), which not only argued that it is constructed around an extremely complex time scheme but also included a series of stylized hourglass diagrams as visual aids.

Despite some of its excesses, however, the New Critical approach to Hardy has remained an influential one. Its concern with the relationship between irony and formal patterning has provided a context for many different kinds of studies of the novels' coherence. Critics who have argued, for example, that the key to the unity of *The Return of the Native* is classical tragedy, like John Paterson and Dale Kramer, have been able to do so within a much more elaborate critical framework than the earliest exponents of that view. Mythic and psychoanalytic approaches have benefited in the same way. Jean R. Brooks, for instance, has examined what she regards as the "poetic" structure of *The Return* in relation to Richard Carpenter's argument that the novel is an ironic treatment of the archetypal myth of the hero.

Peter Casagrande has not only indicated the useful possibilities of a Freudian reading of certain key images in the novel but has also broadened the discussion of figurative structure to include the dimension of characterization, making the highly persuasive and illuminating case that the characters of Christian Cantle and Johnny Nunsuch function, in effect, as narrative counterparts or figurative doubles of Clym Yeobright. This kind of widening of the debate about structure was perhaps initiated in 1966 by David Lodge's chapter on Hardy in his *Language of Fiction*. Lodge was the first critic to suggest the idea that Hardy is not to be regarded as identical with the narrators in his novels. The implication here—that the narrator of *The Return* is not some-how "outside" the structure of the story but an integral aspect of it, like the characters themselves—has led to new ways of exploring the novel's form. It has been a particularly useful starting point for critics like D. R. Schwartz, Dale Kramer, and, of course, J. Hillis Miller.

Miller's *Thomas Hardy: Distance and Desire* (1970) has com-bined the psychoanalytic approach with the pictorial or perceptual one. It amplifies Lodge's argument that there is no "Hardy" in the nov-els, only the many voices and roles he assumes; in this context it ana-lyzes the ways in which the narrators manipulate visual distance in relation to the theme of desire: Miller sees the image of the country dance, with its formal patterns in which the dancers continually sepa-rate and approach each other again, as the central emblem of this rela-tion. Many critics have followed this lead—some focusing on desire, others on distance. T. R. Wright, for example, has examined the struc-ture of *The Return* in the context of its erotic tensions, while J. B. Bullen has concentrated on its visual and perceptual elements, particu-larly with respect to Hardy's knowledge of the techniques of painting. Ian Gregor, in *The Great Web: The Form of Hardy's Major Fiction* (1974), was the first critic to refer to Hardy's basic device of charac-terization as "bifocal"—a term fraught with significant implications for subsequent studies of Hardy's visual method. In an attempt to refine the Jamesian notion of fictional form so as to understand the structure of Hardy's novels, Gregor has suggested that what seems to be incon-sistency in his technique of characterization is in fact complexity—that one kind of perspective on a character is continually modified or undercut by another. In effect, Gregor's study constitutes an attempt to assimilate some of the elements of incongruity in Hardy's fiction to an ideal of formal coherence.

Although this brief survey of the formalist criticism is by no means exhaustive, it is perhaps useful to end it on that note, for it is precisely as a reaction against the idea that incongruity can be assimi-lated to unity in this way that the fourth and most recent critical approach to Hardy originates. In a historical sense, of course, what might be called the antiformalist position on *The Return of the Native* can be seen as going back to some of the earliest reviews and commentaries, which, while acknowledging the novel's power, expressed bewilderment over various kinds of awkwardness and dissonance it also displayed. And later, in dismissing the importance of the novel's formal organization, D. H. Lawrence actually celebrated certain incongruities and inconsistencies, particularly those having to do with characterization: with his idea of the disintegration of "the old stable ego" in fiction, Lawrence anticipated some recent explorations of the fragmentation of personality in Hardy's characters. Similarly, Albert J. Guerard attended closely to the elements of the grotesque and the disproportionate in the novels, while Morton Dauwen Zabel, whose article on Hardy in the *Southern Review* of 1940 was subtitled "The Aesthetic of Incongruity," pointed out their multiple disparities, like the "immensities of scale that wildly exceed the proportions necessary." In effect, Zabel was advocating a nonunitary aesthetic for Hardy's fiction and warning against the formalist tendency to find homogeneity by ignoring incongruity.

In his 1978 *Essay on Hardy* John Bayley challenged the assumption of coherence quite explicitly, arguing that unitary readings of Hardy's novels are reductive and that if there is a single aesthetic principle underlying them it is that of "disunity." J. Hillis Miller had already noted the basic disjunction in Hardy between "desire" and "distance," but he also pointed out that the disjunction goes deeper, for if visual distance establishes desire in the novels, then, given the fact that the prevalent perspective or "gaze" is male, it also divides the characters in a more fundamental way, establishing as well the alienated "otherness" of the women. All this prepared the way for the current dominance of neo-Marxist, deconstructionist, feminist, and neo-psychoanalytic readings of the novels.

Like Lawrence, though in a more thoroughgoing way and in a new ideological context, recent critics like George Wotton, John Goode, and Peter Widdowson have celebrated the disjunctions, discontinuities, and fragmentations in Hardy's "fictional discourses." Deconstructing the texts, rather than demonstrating their wholeness, has become the chief critical aim. In this connection the most intriguing approach has perhaps been the feminist one. Critics like Margaret R. Higonnet, Kristin Brady, Judith Mitchell, Sheila Berger, Penny

Boumelha, and James R. Kincaid, implicitly taking as first principles Zabel's "aesthetic of incongruity" and Miller's perception of the relationship between distance and desire, have illuminated aspects of Hardy's fiction in entirely new ways.

Judith Mitchell, for example, considering the visual or perceptual element in *The Return of the Native,* has pointed out that Eustacia Vye is always an observed object, even when it is Eustacia herself who is doing the observing. For Mitchell, the male gaze, which is the only one shared with the reader, embodies male power and control, so that the women in Hardy are eroticized only by being objectified and hence unable to function as erotic subjects. And while the male gaze confers on women the artificial wholeness of perceived objects, it also reflects a subjectively fragmented sense of male identity. This kind of fragmentation becomes the subject of Marjorie Garson's *Hardy's Fables of Integrity: Woman, Body, Text* (1991), a study that combines feminist ideology with the psychoanalytic method of Jacques Lacan. Besides her highly perceptive and lucid analysis of various submerged anxieties about bodily integrity in Hardy's novels, Garson's treatment of *The Return* brings Mrs. Yeobright into subtextual focus as a remarkably malevolent figure and someone without whom Clym is almost literally lost.

There is much that is new and valuable in the recent criticism. There is also much in it that is simply programmatic and turgid, so that one sometimes has the sense of being preached at rather than of being genuinely persuaded. If Hardy's novels can be said to lack unity of purpose and design, the ideologies underlying the new approach certainly do not. Each of the branches of the newest criticism has, at its worst, a monolithically tendentious quality that tends to preclude flexibility, liveliness of style, and sometimes even a sense of due proportion. Too zealous an ideological commitment can lead to readings as ingeniously perverse as any formerly instigated by the paradox-hunting mania of the older New Criticism—as, for instance, in Rosemarie Morgan's scolding assessment of Diggory Venn as "a powermongering bully and degrader of voluptuous womankind" who "typifies the primitive male censor of female nonconformity."[4]

It is difficult to see where the current discussion of Hardy's fiction is headed. Whatever their shortcomings, the earlier approaches had the virtue of trying as much as possible to take their conceptual frameworks from within the novels themselves. For some reason the aesthetic of incongruity called for by Morton Dauwen Zabel has turned out to be in large part ideologically driven. The trouble with it is not just that it ignores coherence as persistently as the formalist approach has tried to ignore incoherence but that it sees the novels as determined by forces well beyond the imagination of Thomas Hardy and, indeed, well outside literature itself. At any rate, it is devoutly to be wished that some intelligible synthesis of at least the last two approaches touched on in this chapter will soon begin to emerge.

A READING

4

"The Three Women":
Waiting for Saint George

Perhaps there's meaning in it!

Hardy's narrative method in the introductory chapters of *The Return of the Native* seems at first curiously oblique and indirect. It is not just that the plot unfolds slowly—we do not actually meet Clym Yeobright, the eponymous "native," until Book Second—but that certain key plot elements at the story's outset are not made clear. We are presented with a sequence of striking and vivid episodes, but they come in such a way that we do not entirely know at first what to make of them. Nor is it that these early scenes lack significance; on the contrary, they virtually bristle with intimations of meaningfulness. Yet the narrator does not offer the kinds of practical interpretation that might have been expected; he tells us a great deal, but not, initially, exactly what is going on.

When we meet Thomasin Yeobright, for example, she lies in a state of nervous prostration inside Diggory Venn's reddle van, and we, like old Captain Vye, are not at first permitted to see her. Again, our curiosity about what has caused her misery is thwarted, like Captain

Vye's, by Venn's refusal to "gossip" (61). The captain says that he "can guess what has happened" (61) to Thomasin in Anglebury; we of course cannot. Similarly, Eustacia Vye is introduced as no more than a solitary but highly enigmatic "form" (63) seen in dramatic silhouette at the summit of Rainbarrow. But we do not learn more about her for some time, or about what her connection to Thomasin might be. When, together with the assembled local rustics, we catch sight of her curiously private bonfire at Mistover Knap, we are essentially in the position of the perpetually bemused Christian Cantle: "Perhaps," he speculates, "there's meaning in it!" (101).

By the time Mrs. Yeobright appears on the scene we have begun to piece together some parts of the puzzle—the failure of Thomasin's wedding to Damon Wildeve; Eustacia's ambiguous reputation as a dazzling yet sinister beauty and someone suspected locally of witch-craft—but much else remains mysterious. Even Mrs. Yeobright herself initially constitutes something of a mystery. Her attitude to Thomasin's distress seems ambivalent: she evinces much sympathy for her niece in the presence of Diggory Venn, but as soon as the two women are alone together she demands to know "the meaning of this disgraceful performance" (90).

The question of what various kinds of "performance" mean in this novel will later become crucial; in the early chapters of Book First, however, the narrative method is such that *all* meaning seems conspicuously problematic, so that we are continually in the position of trying to make connections left unmade by the narrative, to fill in gaps and elisions deliberately created by it. At one level, what has been omitted turns out to be fairly unremarkable: the Thomasin–Wildeve–Eustacia and the Mrs. Yeobright–Wildeve–Venn triangles belong to a familiar enough tradition of romantic melodra-ma and intrigue. Yet the deviousness of the method suggests that there is more "meaning" here than immediately meets the eye. The alert reader will soon discern a complex but familiar type of love story—but a love story so intensely characterized by frustration and pain as to hint at something larger, some other, more comprehensive dimension of significance. The title of Book First is "The Three Women," and the narrative method suggests that what Thomasin,

Eustacia, and Mrs. Yeobright have in common is the fact that each is mysteriously isolated; it suggests further that this isolation has a resonance that goes beyond anything normally associated with what might be called ordinary or everyday loneliness.

Making connections, the reader becomes increasingly aware in Book First that the world of this novel is one in which the fulfillment of love seems remarkably precarious. Thomasin's situation, the fairly conventional one of damsel-in-distress—in this case that of a woman in effect abandoned at the altar—can be seen as exemplary. This is a society full, so to speak, of absent men, and conversely, of lonely and sad women. When the narrator does begin, in Chapter 6, to observe Eustacia as something other than a dramatic but distant silhouette, he presents her as an almost entirely sexualized creature, a woman crying out—virtually keening—in sheer frustration and longing. We are left in no doubt as to the erotic implications of her lamentation: "she had been existing in a suppressed state, and not in one of languor, or stagnation" (106). Eustacia shudders and becomes aware of Wildeve when he appears as a man unworthy of her; but she also becomes aware of the absence of any other, more appropriate lover, and "indignation spread[s] through her like subterranean heat" (115). We are told of her "flame-like" (119) soul and of "the sad and stifled warmth within her" (120):

> To be loved to madness—such was her great desire. Love was to her the one cordial which could drive away the eating loneliness of her days. And she seemed to long for the abstraction called passionate love more than for any particular lover. . . . Her loneliness deepened her desire. On Egdon, coldest and meanest kisses were at famine prices; and where was a mouth matching hers to be found? (121–22)

Though there is certainly an ironic note in all this—an element in Eustacia of petulant adolescence—the depth of her sense of her abandonment on Egdon Heath is nevertheless convincing and impressive. What is intensely echoed in her situation is not so much Thomasin's distress as Thomasin's current isolation. And there is a significant further echo, fainter but to the same effect, at the first appearance of Mrs.

Yeobright. This "well-known and respected widow" (82) has "something of an estranged mien: the solitude exhaled from the heath was concentrated in this face that had risen from it" (83).

The crucial link, then, among the three women of Book First would seem to be a certain kind of alienation and sadness having to do with absent men. We might be less inclined to see this connection, less likely to emphasize Mrs. Yeobright's widowed state, were it not that the motif of lost husbands and fathers figures so prominently in the conversation of the heath-folk. The irony of the scene at the Quiet Woman Inn derives, of course, from the assumption by Timothy Fairway, Humphrey, and the others that Thomasin is now married, and in the course of what we realize to be an empty, meaningless celebration, Timothy is moved to congratulate Wildeve. "The woman you've got is a dimant" (98), he tells him, which prompts a lengthy communal eulogy of Thomasin's father—"as good a feller as ever lived," Timothy says; "He always had his great indignation ready against anything underhand" (98).

The others go on to remember her father's legendary prowess as a musician, and it becomes clear in the telling that this talent functions as a metaphor for a blazing human (and specifically masculine) vitality, a prodigious creativity that had been extinguished at the height of its powers. Timothy describes him as "a great soul" (99), one of whom strangers would say, "O for such a man in our parish!" (99); Humphrey concludes, "He was the last you'd have expected to drop off in the prime of life" (100). Even at this early stage in *The Return of the Native,* however, the attentive reader cannot help but suspect that Humphrey is wrong—that such a sad end is precisely what should have been expected.

In the world of this novel marriages either fail or come to some other premature end, so that the cynical view of wedded bliss tends to be the wisest. Timothy's amusing recollection of both his own and Humphrey's father's weddings seems to be a kind of normative case in point:

> Ah, Humph, well I can mind when I was married how I zid thy
> father's mark staring me in the face as I went to put down my

name. He and your mother were the couple married just afore we were, and there stood thy father's cross with arms stretched out like a great banging scarecrow. What a terrible black cross that was—thy father's very likeness in en! To save my soul I couldn't help laughing when I zid en, though all the time I was as hot as dog-days, what with the marrying, and what with the woman a-hanging to me, and what with Jack Changley and a lot more chaps grinning at me through church window. But the next moment a strawmote would have knocked me down, for I called to mind that if thy father and mother had had high words once, they'd been at it twenty times since they'd been man and wife, and I zid myself as the next poor stunpoll to get into the same mess. (73–74)

The effect is, of course, primarily comic, but there are darker undertones as well, and not only in the implication of the inevitability of antagonism and discord: Humphrey's father seems no longer to be present, and the image of his "signature"—the terrible black cross that somehow embodies his likeness—is both somber and ominous.

Just about the only visible father figure in *The Return of the Native* is Grandfer Cantle, and he, too, is conceived in essentially comic terms. The comedy depends largely on the fact that Grandfer Cantle operates as a kind of "humor" among the rustics. A virtually Dickensian grotesque, this old man's humorous "signature" is his repetitive boasting about his prowess in his youth as both a lover and a soldier. Here at least, it seems, we have one man of great vitality who has not dropped off in the prime of life. The basic joke, however, is that Grandfer Cantle keeps plaintively insisting that this prowess of his has not been diminished in the slightest by the passage of time, that he is still in effect a lusty young spark. And certainly he does evince a surprising liveliness as a singer and a dancer. The trouble is that his obsessiveness and self-absorption produce an effect not only bizarre but often slightly ghoulish, as if Grandfer Cantle were forever perversely declaring himself exempt from certain laws of nature. Always engaged in a form of special pleading on his own behalf, he has no time for his son; and although Christian Cantle amounts to another comic humor in his own right, we cannot help but feel that his equally obsessive anxiety and fearfulness have at least something to do with the fact of his father's overbearing nature, that the two are really opposite sides of a single coin. Christian seems to have spent his life in his father's shadow; the standing joke about his impotence has its dark and pathetic side as well.

Christian's ineffectuality, his definitive lack of manliness, is as resonant in relation to the motif of lonely or alienated women as are the fragmentary tales about lost husbands and marriages that have come to grief. One of the links that we can hardly fail to make among the various characters and incidents in Book First has to do with the failure of love in a very specific sense: the pervasiveness of a certain spiritual barrenness. From the outset, almost every episode seems to suggest that the great promise of life somehow invariably turns to dust, that it is in the nature of things for expectations of fulfillment to be frustrated. It might be argued that this theme is subverted or at any rate counterpointed by the great initial blaze of bonfires—the human assertion of the power of life in the face of a wintry darkness—or by the insistent energy of eros implicit in the rustics' dance among their bonfire's embers. But there is also the muted sense of a general whistling in the dark about all this, the kind of note that marks Grandfer Cantle's efforts always to appear youthful. Even the imperious summons of Eustacia's fire results only in the appearance of Damon Wildeve, a lover conspicuously unengaging. And the spiritually empty Wildeve is the lover—precisely because he is the only one in sight—who seems to epitomize the essential aridity of the world of love in Book First.

In another sense, of course, this quality of barrenness is epitomized not so much by any of the characters as by Egdon Heath itself. Among the various pieces of the puzzle that we are implicitly invited to assemble in the early chapters, the setting appears to constitute a particularly significant item. Nothing is so strikingly imbued with the sense of meaningfulness as Egdon Heath. Many critics have in fact felt that Hardy's treatment of the heath, especially in Book First, is too portentous. Certainly, one of the effects of the account that takes up all of Chapter 1 is to suggest the narrator's need to establish unequivocally from the outset that this vast tract of inarable land resonates with symbolic meaning. The portentousness derives from the fact that, initially at least, what the heath "means" seems less complicated than the narrator wants to allow. A lonely and inhospitable place, it is characterized primarily by its "darkness" (53), and thus by all the ominous or sinister associations of night. It wears "the appearance of an instalment of night which had taken up its place before its astronomical hour was come" (53), and is in fact described as "a near relation of night" (53). As an "untameable" (56) wilderness—"Civilization was its enemy" (56)—it has a certain natural sublimity and somber inviolability, but in mythic terms what this suggests is the idea of nature as something alien and forbidding, a dark parody of Eden, a paradise "lost" in the sense that it is, from the human point of view, essentially infertile or inaccessible.

An emblem perhaps, then, of what Christianity would regard as nature in its fallen state, the heath is also evidently a "lower" world in even older mythic contexts: it contains an ancient Celtic burial mound, Rainbarrow, and is perceived as a "Titanic form" (54) buried or chained in Hades and frequently referred to as "Tartarean" (86). So the heath is a kind of underworld, its darkness like that of hell itself, and its most obvious association is with death. This pattern of symbolism is, however, not quite so unambiguous as one might at first expect.

Although Egdon is seen in terms chiefly of its deathliness, it does have its own peculiar vitality. At night, we are told, "[t]he place became full of a watchful intentness . . . for when other things sank brooding to sleep the heath appeared slowly to awake and listen" (54). Indeed, the title of Chapter 1 refers to its unchanging "face," as if it were a living creature. And the paradox is soon elaborated quite explicitly:

> there was that in the condition of the heath itself which resembled protracted and halting dubiousness. It was the quality of the repose appertaining to the scene. This was not the repose of actual stagnation, but the apparent repose of incredible slowness. A condition of healthy life so nearly resembling the torpor of death is a noticeable thing of its sort; to exhibit the inertness of the desert, and at the same time to be exercising powers akin to those of the meadow, and even of the forest, awakened in those who thought of it the attentiveness usually engendered by understatement and reserve. (62)

Figuratively, the heath is at once dead and alive. There is something in it, in other words, that echoes the condition of human isolation:

> It was at present a place perfectly accordant with man's nature— neither ghastly, hateful, nor ugly: neither commonplace, unmeaning, nor tame; but, like man, slighted and enduring; and withal singularly colossal and mysterious in its swarthy monotony. As with persons who have long lived apart, solitude seemed to look out of its countenance. It had a lonely face, suggesting tragical possibilities. (55)

The paradox becomes most clearly intelligible when it is seen in relation to one of the strands in the pattern of mythic significance already alluded to: the heath as an emblem of a "fallen" nature. In that context it is neither quite a dead desert nor a living meadow but, rather, a wasteland symbolizing the type of life-in-death which, in the Christian tradition, characterizes postlapsarian human experience.

Other paradoxes with respect to the heath become intelligible only in the same context. On the one hand, for instance, Egdon is an "untameable Ishmaelitish thing" (56), an earth that cannot be cultivated, a place set apart from all human aspiration; yet on the other, Timothy, Humphrey, Sam, and the rest do manage to extract their livelihood from it. At times, indeed, the local people actually seem to be not just in harmony with the heath but even physically assimilated to it, as when we first glimpse them: "Every individual was so involved in furze by his method of carrying the faggots that he appeared like a bush on legs till he had thrown them down" (65). And later, when Diggory Venn spies on the second clandestine meeting between Wildeve and Eustacia, he camouflages himself with turves, so that as he crawls toward them, "it was as though he burrowed underground" (136).

The basis of the affinity between humanity and the "Ishmaelitish thing" is that humanity itself is doomed, according to one of the myths that Hardy invokes, to a kind of perpetual exile and isolation, an "underground" form of life that is also, figuratively, a form of death. In this context, Eustacia Vye's predicament becomes exemplary:

Egdon was her Hades, and since coming there she had imbibed much of what was dark in its tone, though inwardly and eternally unreconciled thereto. Her appearance accorded well with this smouldering rebelliousness, and the shady splendour of her beauty was the real surface of the sad and stifled warmth within her. A true Tartarean dignity sat upon her brow. (119–20)

Although entirely alienated from her surroundings, it is as if Eustacia has also been absorbed by them: "Like the summer condition of the place around her, she was an embodiment of the phrase, 'a populous solitude'—apparently so listless, void, and quiet, she was really busy and full" (121).

In effect, the logic underlying these paradoxes depends on the way Hardy not only invokes but also conflates two distinct mythological traditions: we have, in one, the biblical story about the fall from Eden as a descent into a kind of life that can look more like a living death, and, in the other, the classical legend of Hades, in which the dead survive in various degrees of anguish as shades. Egdon is the fallen world, but it is also Eustacia's Hades in the sense that she is in the position of Persephone trapped in the underworld—a figure who constitutes the very embodiment of the life force exiled to the world of death. Eustacia is the "queen of night" as Persephone is the classical queen of hell. And this conflation of Christian and pagan symbolism can also be seen in the novel's structure of cyclical seasonal imagery. The narrative begins at the turning of the year in November. This marks the beginning of a descent into the darkness and death of winter, the season linked to the kind of aridity and despair that we have noted. At least two of the three women of Book First are waiting, without much hope, for the redemption and significance that love can bring, and their situation seems to deteriorate rather than improve. At the very nadir of that process, just before Christmas in fact, Clym Yeobright returns. To clarify his mythic role at this season, Book Second is entitled "The Arrival": Clym is to be a savior, a man who will redeem the dead land through the power of his love.

Once we have begun to discern the outlines of this biblical pattern, the significance of other things that may have seemed obscure in

Book First starts to become clearer. In the strikingly odd matter of Diggory Venn's redness, for instance, the effect is again at first glance paradoxical. The almost ineradicable stain suggests an affinity between Diggory and the heath: he, too, is "Ishmaelitish," a lonely wanderer indelibly marked by the color of blood; there are echoes of Cain in this, so that he seems to be a walking emblem of original sin. But of course the general thrust of this interpretation also seems to be increasingly at odds with what we learn of his character. His rescue of Thomasin in Anglebury, his devoted fidelity to her, and his subsequent machinations on her behalf make him the most (almost the only) sympathetic male character in Book First. Initially, Diggory even looks as if he might be the novel's hero—Hardy's version of a Spenserian Redcross Knight to Thomasin's Una. The paradox of Diggory is resolved, however, in the context of the novel's structure of biblical allusion. If the manner of Clym's later arrival makes him into a kind of Christ figure, then Diggory can logically be regarded as his prototype. In biblical typology, Christ is the "second" Adam, who redeems the sinfulness of the first. Diggory's redness, then, echoes the original Adam's name, the etymological derivation of which is "red earth." His affinity with the heath has to do with his symbolically "fallen" status, and with the consequent limitations inherent in the power of his love, attested to by the fact that his feelings for Thomasin are unrequited.

There are various pagan versions of the Christian story about a savior who comes to redeem the world in the dead of winter. Many critics have pointed out that *The Return of the Native* is informed by what amounts to a fertility or vegetation myth in which a dark, barren land is restored to life by an archetypal hero associated with the sun.[5] Jean R. Brooks, for instance, offers this summary of Clym Yeobright's career:

> His originality is recognized at an early age, he serves his apprenticeship in a foreign land guarding treasure, and becomes possessed of deeper knowledge which he wishes to pass on to his people. His temporary withdrawal from the world suggests the initiation of a sun-god-hero into a religious cult. He returns to his birthplace, a dark and fallen world (Tartarus, the prison of the

exiled Titans) but is not really recognized. He is diverted from his quest by a dark and beautiful enchantress against the wishes of his goddess mother, undergoes a period of spiritual trial and is symbolically blinded, like Oedipus and Milton's Satan, so that he may achieve true insight. (Brooks, 29–30)

But all the critics, including Brooks, agree that Hardy's treatment of this type of legend is deeply ironic. Clym is as flawed a sun hero as he is a Christ figure, and his quest inevitably ends in failure.

Persuasive as these particular mythic readings are, they have the curious effect of simultaneously bringing us closer to understanding the text, and yet distancing us from it. They do not quite come to terms with the intensely localized quality of Hardy's universe, with the specific density of all the details that go to make it up. Egdon is certainly "dark and fallen," but more specifically, as we have seen, it is a wasteland; more specifically still, it is a wasteland whose barrenness seems to be reflected in the failure—as suggested by the isolated or distressed women and the absent or inadequate men—of human love. Similarly, although it seems valid and useful to assert that Diggory's redness links him with the figure of Adam, this also amounts to a generalized and moralized significance that is at odds with the actual texture of the novel. The red stain has another symbolic dimension—a visual, pictorial one.

What we are initially made aware of in the novel's first episode is not the redness of Diggory Venn but the whiteness of the road along which he travels. This is an old Roman road that, unlike the maze of crisscrossing paths on the heath itself, virtually bisects it in a straight line; even in the gathering darkness of Egdon at the end of Chapter 1, "the white surface of the road remained almost as clear as ever" (57). Its very straightness makes the road an image of the kind of civilization that, we have been told, is Egdon's "enemy" (56): in the midst of this wilderness, the road signifies the distinctly human realm of rationality and order. At the same time, however, it becomes an image, seen from the perspective of Captain Vye, suggesting indefiniteness and weariness: "Before him stretched the long, laborious road, dry, empty and white" (58). This emptiness is, of course, evocative of the aridity in the human realm that we have noted, and it is echoed in the very appearance of the retired naval officer. The old man is "white-headed as a mountain, bowed in the shoulders, and faded in general aspect" (58). But all this arid whiteness soon becomes merely the background against which he and we glimpse the distant "lurid red" (58) spot of Diggory's van, and then the adjacent redness of Diggory himself moving beside it.

Red and white are the colors usually associated in literature with love. When Captain Vye learns that the distressed person in the van is a young woman, he tells Diggory, "That would have interested me forty years ago" (60). The implication is clear: a once vigorous young man, linked for much of his life to the symbolic fertility of the sea, has been reduced to the impotence of old age. (We meet a variation of the same motif later in the relationship between Grandfer Cantle and Christian.) And if that impotence is visually expressed by all the dry and faded whiteness in the picture, then the lurid redness of Diggory expresses the erotic fervor of a young man's love. Diggory is still a frustrated lover, of course, and his rescue effort has only a limited and temporary efficacy. But the visual organization of the scene goes beyond the theme of frustrated desire to become a kind of emblematic encoding of nothing less than a familiar national legend: the red shape seen against a white background suggests the heraldic banner of Saint George, the red cross of the patron saint of England.

For the specific version of the archetypal sun-hero story hovering just behind the action of the novel, the myth that merges with the Christian one about a redeemer who comes to restore life, is the legend of Saint George and the dragon. This has been succinctly summarized in a different context by Northrop Frye:

> In this legend an old and impotent king rules over a wasteland oppressed by a sea monster who demands human victims. Already we see a cluster of metaphorical identifications. The land is waste because the king is impotent, the fertility of the land and the virility of the king being linked by sympathetic magic. The monster from the sea inevitably turns up when the land and the king have lost their power, because he is another

aspect of sterility. The victims provided for his dinner are chosen by lot, and eventually the lot falls on the king's daughter. At that point the hero arrives, also from over the sea; he kills the dragon, releases the daughter, and becomes the next king by marrying her . . . . As a myth of renewal, its general shape is clear enough: the hero is the reviving power of spring and the monster and old king the outgrown forces of apathy and impotence in a symbolic winter.[6]

Many elements of this myth appear in the novel in virtually undisplaced form. The symbolism of the wasteland and the related motifs of barrenness and impotence are indeed conspicuous. Certainly, Captain Vye, that "decayed" (59) naval officer, can be seen as a type of the fisher king; and by the end of Book First there is much excited anticipation on Egdon over the impending arrival of Clym Yeobright, the hero who actually does come from over the sea and who, in Book Second, is to be explicitly linked to the figure of Saint George. The implication is that Clym will supplant Diggory in the role of heroic rescuer. As regards the role of the prospective female victim, however, Hardy's treatment of the story arranges matters somewhat differently.

Two candidates seem to be offered in Book First—Thomasin Yeobright and Eustacia Vye. This binary arrangement, the division of the role of heroine between two young women, one fair and the other dark, constitutes a conventional "doubling" device in Victorian romantic fiction. The point is that the hero must usually choose between them, and he often makes the wrong choice, as Clym seems to do in this novel.There has always been a vague expectation among the inhabitants of Egdon Heath that Clym will marry Thomasin. But his absence abroad has gone on for too long. In a letter rejecting Diggory's proposal of marriage two years prior to the events described in Book First, Thomasin wrote, "It makes me very sad . . . for I like you very much, and I always put you next to my cousin Clym in my mind" (133). Clym's place there, however, has now been taken by Damon Wildeve, and as Timothy Fairway says, "What's the good of . . . Clym a-coming home after the deed's done? He should have come afore, if so he wanted to stop it, and marry her himself" (78).

In any case, even though Thomasin's wedding in Anglebury has been bungled (to put Wildeve's motives there in the most charitable light), Clym will choose Eustacia Vye. Eustacia is a much more ambiguous and passionate young woman than Thomasin, almost (though, as we shall see, not altogether) an operatic enchantress, and it is the magnetic intensity of her romantically longing nature that will draw Clym to her. Her isolation is profounder than Thomasin's, and the sheer passion of her rebelliousness against the heath perhaps suggests more clearly the extent to which the whole world of Egdon seems to be in the grip of an overwhelming aridity. Still, her distress, while different in degree, is of the same kind as Thomasin's—the kind emblematically summed up in the figure of the "quiet" (because headless!) woman portrayed on the signboard of Wildeve's inn: that of being doomed to a condition of life that, figuratively, is a form of animate death.

Both women are fatherless and hence, or so the convention goes, vulnerable, though Eustacia's grandfather clearly functions as a surrogate paternal type. But in relation to his unhappy granddaughter, Captain Vye is conspicuously remote and ineffectual. He lives as much as possible in his own seafaring past. The high bank outside Mistover Knap suggests the deck of a fortified ship, and the chief attraction of the heath to him is the way in which it resembles the ocean. This association of Egdon with the sea is in fact hinted at in the first chapter:

> The great inviolate place had an ancient permanence which the sea cannot claim. Who can say of a particular sea that it is old? Distilled by the sun, kneaded by the moon, it is renewed in a year, in a day, or in an hour. The sea changed, the fields changed, the rivers, the villages, and the people changed, yet Egdon remained. (56)

The heath is in fact more like the sea than the sea itself. The rhetorical basis of the comparison is Egdon's apparent immutability, the sense of an indefinite rolling expanse on which "time makes but little impression." And it is against this static, unchanging quality of the place that Eustacia's hourglass and telescope can be seen as her private symbols of rebellion. Her need for the hourglass has to do with her need literally to *see* that time does actually pass on Egdon, to reassure herself that there is indeed a larger world not governed by stasis, in which any "impression" made by time would be at least a guarantee of vitality. The telescope seems to be her private perceptual weapon against the analogous spatial manifestation of the same stasis: her way of trying to counter an all-encompassing and monotonous remoteness of prospect.

If Mistover Knap looks rather like a ship at sea, it is as if each of the other two houses in Book First were a lonely cottage perched precariously at the shore. Blooms-End, as its name suggests, seems to sit at the very edge of the uncultivable world, and "Wildeve's Patch" (87), the property adjoining the Quiet Woman Inn, is described in terms that suggest the painful difficulty of the reclamation of the arable from the inarable. It is

> a plot of land redeemed from the heath, and after long and laborious years brought into cultivation. The man who had discovered that it could be tilled died of the labour: the man who succeeded him in possession ruined himself in fertilizing it. Wildeve came like Amerigo Vespucci, and received the honours due to those who had gone before. (87)

This passage tells us much about Wildeve himself. A failed engineer, he is associated with the mechanical barrenness and spiritual emptiness of the modern industrial world, which, in Hardy's fiction, always seems to threaten to overwhelm the organic vitality of rural Wessex. In this respect Diggory Venn functions not only as Wildeve's rival but as his antithesis: as a reddle man, Diggory represents a way of life that is almost extinct ("reddle" is the red-ochre stain used to mark sheep); he is the by now virtually archaic embodiment of that same natural vitality.

To all this it might be objected that Diggory is closely identified in the novel with the inarable landscape of Egdon Heath; that the heath, not the world beyond it, is the chief figurative embodiment of aridity; and that this wasteland cannot be like the sea if, as we have suggested, the sea is a symbol of fertility. What these objections do not take into account is the binary character of this kind of archetypal imagery. The sea can indeed be a symbol of life, but it can also be one of death: its meaning is always determined by the context in which it is perceived. We noted the paradox earlier in which Egdon may be said to look, depending on who is doing the looking, either alive or dead—precisely because of the basic figurative duality implicit in the condition of life-in-death. For Eustacia, the heath is a prison and a hell because it is associated with her perception of the elements of captivity and deathliness inherent in her lonely situation. Later, on his return, Clym sees the place in a quite different way, but by then Eustacia's point of view has acquired a certain narrative primacy. So while the sea may be linked in some contexts to the idea of an abundant fertility, Egdon resembles the sea in this novel primarily in the sense that it represents a virtually alien element, one that sometimes seems capable of engulfing all human life.

In Book First two major symbols, elemental and also binary, are set against the heath's darkness and aridity. Fire and water (fresh rather than sea water now) can both be seen, depending again on context, as either creative or destructive. These natural elements constitute two of the metaphorical organizing principles in the novel as a whole, and in Book First fire and water are on the side of life. Both are closely linked to Eustacia, to her rebelliousness and her longing.

With her "flame-like" soul, Eustacia, consistently described in terms of heat and light, is a quintessentially fiery character. Even when her fires are banked, they have the kind of smouldering, subterranean quality that we associate with the possibility of volcanic eruption. Her energies are extravagant and prodigal. Her slow-burning bonfire in Book First is fueled by her grandfather's winter supply of hardwood; when he plaintively admonishes her for wasting it—"My precious thorn roots, the rarest of all firing, that I laid by on purpose for Christmas" (110)—the sense is that what is virtually being consumed is the remaining store of life in Captain Vye himself. His rebuke has no force, however, for Eustacia is "absolute queen here" (110).

The brightness of Eustacia's bonfire is justified by virtue of its being "Promethean" (67), figuratively linked, in other words, to the theft of divine fire perpetrated by one of the classical Titans who was exiled to just such a "Tartarean" darkness as Egdon's. In the novel's romantic context, the crime of Prometheus is itself justified because it is an affirmation of the worth and power of human life in the face of death. This "spontaneous Promethean rebelliousness" is in fact evoked by all the bonfires on Egdon on 5 November, Guy Fawkes Day, "against the fiat that this recurrent season shall bring foul times, cold darkness, misery and death. Black chaos comes, and the fettered gods of the earth say, Let there be light" (67). For Eustacia, this gesture of defiance also signifies the force of her desire and longing; her fire is a signal and a desperate summons to a former lover.

The constellation of bonfires shining in the darkness at the story's outset is associated not only with the erotic but with the macabre and the subterranean. The chiaroscuro effect of the first detailed description of the rustics seems to transform them almost literally into denizens of the underworld:

> The brilliant lights and sooty shades which struggled upon [their] skin and clothes . . . caused their lineaments and general contours to be drawn with Dureresque vigour and dash. . . . [A]s the nimble flames towered, nodded, and swooped through the surrounding air, the blots of shade and flakes of light upon the countenances of the group changed shape and position endlessly. All was unstable; quivering as leaves, evanescent as lightning. Shadowy eye-sockets, deep as those of a death's head, suddenly turned into pits of lustre: a lantern-jaw was cavernous, then it was shining; wrinkles were emphasized to ravines, or obliterated entirely by a changed ray. Nostrils were dark wells; sinews in old necks were gilt mouldings; things with no particular polish on them were glazed; bright objects, such as the tip of a furze-hook . . . were as glass; eyeballs glowed like little lanterns. Those whom Nature had depicted as merely quaint became grotesque, the grotesque became preternatural; for all was in extremity. (67–68)

And when they begin their dance among the sparks and embers, the celebratory sexual quality in the sudden pairings and wild movements is perceived as "demoniac" (81)—"a whirling of dark shapes amid a boiling confusion of sparks, which leapt around the dancers as high as their waists" (81). Again, the sense is of an "underground" vitality, a vision of energy as a quasi-infernal force somehow dispersed or scattered beneath the surface of the earth.

What it suggests is the kind of embryonic life that planted seeds have, the fire of genuine human vitality taking the form of something like a "confusion" of chthonic sparks. The image perhaps brings to mind the first section of T. S. Eliot's *The Waste Land,* in which the chief fear of the seedlike "dead"—all those who have been "buried"—is that of being dug up again and restored to life. Such an association is not quite as free and fanciful as it might seem: Eliot's poem, published 44 years after the publication of *The Return of the Native,* is also constructed on the basis of the legend of Saint George and the fisher king; and to the extent that its structure depends as well on the elemental symbols of fire and water, *The Waste Land* has certain intriguing affinities with this novel.

In Book First of *The Return of the Native* the imagery of water plays a less prominent part than that of fire, and certainly much less significant a role than it does later on in the novel—the literal aridity of the heath in November being less definitive than its darkness. Apart from the allusions to the sea, however, the first book does feature one important water image: the reference to the pool that has formed in the ditch below the bank at Mistover Knap. Little Johnny Nunsuch is instructed by Eustacia to listen for the sound of a frog jumping into this pond; if he hears such a noise he must let her know, she tells him, "because it is a sign of rain" (110). In fact, of course, Eustacia is anticipating the arrival of Wildeve. Like her bonfire, the pool functions as part of an established system of signals between clandestine lovers. Her remark is worth mentioning here, not only because the pool's associations are with the world of eros, but also because it represents the first adumbration of the great climactic rainstorm in Book Fifth, during the course of which Eustacia will drown in a local weir. The action of a story that begins with erotic and Promethean fire will end with a nearly apocalyptic deluge.

To recapitulate, then: the world of love presented in Book First is characterized by a radical disjunction between desire and fulfilment; each of the three women on Egdon Heath is in some sense isolated and alienated; and in establishing such a climate of barrenness Hardy creates the appropriate mythic context for the impending arrival of a redeemer, a hero from over the sea who will somehow renew the very sources of love and life. At almost the same time that he invokes this myth, however, Hardy carefully undermines it. We have seen that his narrative method at the outset involves a deliberate temporary withholding from the reader of certain crucial narrative facts and links; it also involves a way of telling the story that depends on the continuous alternation of two quite distinct visual points of view—a procedure that turns out to be structurally subversive.

There is a curious doubleness in the narrative perspective in the novel's early chapters, a twofold way of seeing exemplified perhaps most clearly in the gradual revelation of the character of Eustacia Vye. In the first place, we glimpse Eustacia from a great distance—the cinematic analogue would be the panoramic long shot—and it is suddenly as if the narrator had removed himself from his story. Instead, we get the perspective of "an imaginative stranger," a hypothetical observer who watches her silhouette as it rises up from the great burial mound of Rainbarrow and whose "first instinct . . . might have been to suppose it the person of one of the Celts who built the barrow" (62). This distant sight may be enigmatic, but it is certainly rich in implication, perhaps suggesting, for example, that the figure has actually emerged from the world of the dead. Whatever the author's intention, however, the scene is clearly meaningful—and meaningful in a highly stylized, iconographic way: "Above the plain rose the hill, above the hill rose the barrow, and above the barrow rose the figure. Above the figure was nothing that could be mapped elsewhere than on a celestial globe" (63).

The issue of "meaning" is explicitly invoked shortly afterwards, when the arrival of the rustics causes the figure to vanish: "The only intelligible meaning in this sky-backed performance was that the woman had no relation to the forms who had taken her place" (63); and again we have the detached viewpoint of the "observer" (63), whose "imagination . . . clung by preference to that vanished, solitary figure, as to something more interesting, more important, more likely to have a history worth knowing than these newcomers" (63–64). It is not just that Hardy wants to arouse our curiosity about Eustacia, but also that he is concerned to establish a certain kind of significative context for her: whatever *her* "performance" might mean, this remote figure seems to belong to the world of high romance, or even to myth.

Our next view is slightly less remote—Eustacia is now crying out mysteriously from the top of the barrow—yet still far enough for the romantic/mythic context to persist. This impression is heightened, in fact, by the famous "Queen of Night" chapter, in which Eustacia becomes a beautiful but cruel moon goddess—"Artemis, Athena, or Hera" (119). But when the narrative perspective finally shifts to the fictional equivalent of the cinematic medium close-up, Eustacia begins to look less sublime. The context changes, too. From up close she now seems at times not only more ordinary but absurdly supercilious and willful, a spoiled child even, given to poses and imperious foot-stomping. The context has been transformed, in other words, to that of psychological realism.

What concerns us at present is not so much that Eustacia is a moody and contradictory character as that the context established in the medium close-up mode tends to undermine the one evoked earlier by the panoramic long shot. The process, in which whole realms of potentially "mythic" meaning are considerably modified by the conventions and exigencies of mimetic realism, is perfectly summed up in the final visual account that we are given of Eustacia in Book First. "She placed her hand to her forehead," the narrator announces, "and breathed heavily," which leads us to expect yet another manifestation of the lofty queen-of-night persona: "and then her rich, romantic lips parted under that homely impulse—a yawn" (157). Perhaps Eustacia is after all simply bored, the intensity of her romantic longing no more than self-dramatization and posturing. But of course the technique is not so simple or reductive. In his future dealings with Eustacia, the narrator will revert again and again to the mythic mode; when he does undermine it, he will rarely do so quite as unambiguously or comically.

Such a method is nevertheless subversive—a procedure always close to the technique of parody—and this type of ironic subversion lies at the very heart of the novel's structure. Our reading of Eustacia by the end of Book First includes the sense that she does not quite manage to live up to the various mythic roles assigned to her. In our reading of Clym Yeobright throughout the rest of the novel, this same sense becomes even more acute. Clym does not fulfill the expectations created for him in Book First, and he turns out to have been badly miscast in the part of Saint George. The specific reasons for his failure as a hero will become clearer later on, but what we can say of him here is that there is a basic and profound irony in his obsessive scheme to improve life for the inhabitants of Egdon Heath. His educational project is sterile from the outset, reflecting a flawed power of vision, a certain imaginative blindness in Clym himself, because it tries to address the wrong kind of problem. The real problem is not Egdon's intellectual or cultural backwardness but the more radical type of barrenness suggested by the lonely isolation and unhappiness of the three women. The problem's figurative terms of reference, that is to say, have to do with some fundamental impoverishment of love. Clym Yeobright does become a husband before he becomes a teacher, but as a heroic or "mythic" lover he is disastrously inadequate.

Clym's psychological passivity has been much discussed by critics, and a few have noted that, as the novel proceeds, this characteristic seems increasingly to have a sexual dimension as well. Irving Howe, for instance, remarks that

> the decay of Clym's sight also suggests a diminished virility. Eustacia need not shear the locks of this fretful husband, who can at best be stubborn when his need is to be strong; it is quite enough that he declines into a leaden figure doing his mindless chores and withdrawing into heavy sexless sleep.[7]

Similarly, in considering Christian Cantle as a narrative foil to Clym, Peter J. Casagrande says,

> Most striking . . . is the connection between Clym's asceticism . . . and Christian's sexual impotency. . . . [Christian] is the instrument of Hardy's carefully contrived attempt to show that sexual immaturity, perhaps even sexual impotency, is an important element in Clym's character. (Casagrande, 125–26)

At the literal level, the evidence of this kind of sexual dysfunction may not be conclusive; at the figurative level, however, there can be no doubt of it. The ultimate irony in *The Return of the Native* is that, while invoking the legend of Saint George and the dragon, a story about a battle against sterility, the novel presents as its protagonist a character who is himself in effect impotent.

This leaves the admittedly large question as to the identity of the dragon. There are of course no actual monsters in realistic fiction; there are plenty of virtual ones, though, and in this sense *The Return of the Native* offers various possible candidates. Many of the characters— Eustacia Vye, Damon Wildeve, the deluded Susan Nunsuch, and others—behave monstrously at times. Monstrousness could also be imputed, as it so often is in considerations of Hardy, to fate or accident or the indifference or malevolence of the cosmos. But as we shall see, the only intelligible short answer to the question is that the monster is Egdon Heath itself.

5

"The Arrival": Inside the White Palings

Inside is Paradise.

Robert Heilman remarks that in Book Second Eustacia Vye "thinks of Clym as a deliverer."[8] While this thought, occurring to her as it does before she has actually met him, can be seen as exemplifying Eustacia's immaturity and romantic narcissism, it is at the same time not so very far removed from what everyone else on Egdon Heath thinks as well. Clym's arrival coincides with that of Christmas, and the news of it is treated in the Quiet Woman Inn "as if it were of national importance" (158). "Coming across the water" (163) from Paris to Budmouth, he is discussed in terms appropriate to a legendary hero even by such down-to-earth characters as Humphrey and Sam. Indeed, it is Humphrey's attempt to convey to Captain Vye some sense of the local legend of Clym's unique brilliance that leads the eavesdropping Eustacia to think of him as a savior in the first place. Soon afterward she has a dream about a mysterious knight in shining armor—and "shining" is the operative word in this context. If Eustacia is figuratively dead, imprisoned in the Tartarean darkness of Egdon, then Clym—his reputed brilliance embodied for her by the "blazing great [diamond] business"

(162) managed by him in Paris—represents the fabulous light that will revive and lead her out of it.

The significance of Clym's assigned role in this respect is suggested allegorically by the Saint George play, into which Eustacia actually manages to insinuate herself as a clandestine actor. The traditional Christmas mummers' play deals with a different phase of the Saint George myth from the one that informs the novel—that of the hero as Christian scourge of the infidel in the Holy Land rather than as dragon slayer—but it is no less clearly focused on the theme of death and resurrection. In the course of various enacted battles both Christian and pagan knights are slain, the issue being decided only after Saint George has managed to kill the wicked Turkish knight, played by Eustacia herself. In all versions of the play, including this one, however, the dead characters are magically brought back to life at the end by a "Doctor" with a secret regenerative potion. And it is on precisely this motif of universal revivification that the figurative structure of Book Second depends.

Conceived quite specifically by Eustacia as a man who might "deliver her soul" (187), Clym is linked even more powerfully in her mind with the image of a life-restoring sun. The Christmas party at Blooms-End affords her the opportunity of actually "seeing the man whose influence was penetrating her like summer sun" (180); and later, after the "deity" that "shone out of him like a ray" (195) has been made visible to her, we learn that, in contrast to Clym, "Wildeve had at present the rayless outline of the sun through smoked glass" (203). Sunlight is crucial in Book Second, and not only in its effect on Eustacia: in the apple loft at Blooms-End it falls on Thomasin "so . . . that it almost seemed to shine through her" (166); similarly, just prior to her wedding, we are told that "The sun . . . made a mirror of Thomasin's hair" (215). It is as if she has been utterly illuminated by this light, totally revealed; and although the sun animates Eustacia as well, her renewed liveliness is as characteristically oblique and devious as Thomasin's is transparent and honest.

The sun's kindling effect connects it, of course, to the fire imagery in the elemental fire/water pattern we have noted. In Book Second the images of fuel and fire continue to have the metaphorical resonance of erotic awakening. Just after her first glimpse of Clym, for example, Eustacia returns home in a state of high excitement to find her grandfather "enjoying himself over the fire, raking about the ashes and exposing the red-hot surface of the turves, so that their lurid glare irradiated the chimney-corner with the hues of a furnace" (173). "'Why is it,'" she asks—"coming forward and stretching her soft hands over the warmth"—"'that we are never friendly with the Yeobrights?'" (173). The scene is set in the same chimney corner where Eustacia had first overheard Humphrey's encomium of Clym, as he and Sam stacked Captain Vye's supply of winter fuel, and the fuel house itself is where Eustacia first bewitches the adolescent Charley and where the mummers rehearse their play. Eustacia's dream about the knight in armor is described as "fuel" for her "newly kindled fervour" (174), a type of fire whose mythic significance is indicated in the more whimsical account of the blaze inside the settle at the Blooms-End Christmas party: "Inside is Paradise. Not a symptom of a draught disturbs the air; the sitters' backs are as warm as their faces, and songs and old tales are drawn from the occupants by the comfortable heat, like fruit from melon-plants in a frame" (193).

The homely exoticism of this picture—the sense of a quasi-tropical profusion of life teeming paradoxically in the depths of a Wessex winter—has its counterpart as well in Hardy's deployment of water imagery in Book Second. The news of Clym's coming inspires such "visions" in Eustacia, for instance, that "She could never have believed in the morning that her colourless inner world would before night become as animated as water under a microscope, and that without the arrival of a single visitor" (164). Again the mythic source of this teeming inner abundance would seem to be Edenic: in her dream she feels "like a woman in Paradise" (174), and the pool into which she dives with her knight, both of them emerging "somewhere beneath an iridescent hollow arched with rainbows" (174), echoes the traditional biblical account of the source of the river of life.

The paradisal motif is itself, of course, paradoxical. Egdon Heath is the dead land to which life must be restored, and yet even Eustacia is capable of seeing or at least dreaming of it in Edenic terms. Narrative meaning is always determined by narrative point of view, and the perspective in the dream is that of a woman aflame with her own need for love. In fact, the Edenic motif is no less ubiquitous in Book Second than the image of the revivifying sun. The heath is presented at the very outset of Book Second, almost as if in controversion of the narrator's account at the beginning of Book First and of Eustacia's normal view of it, as a paradisal garden:

> here, away from comparisons, shut in by the stable hills, among which mere walking had the novelty of pageantry, and where any man could imagine himself to be Adam without the least difficulty, [certain ephemeral operations] attracted the attention of every bird within eyeshot, every reptile not yet asleep, and set the surrounding rabbits curiously watching from hillocks at a safe distance. (161)

The scene looks like a pastoral idyll, yet the "ephemeral operations" turn out to be the activities of human beings at work—Humphrey and Sam stacking fuel for Captain Vye—which is not, from the human point of view, particularly idyllic at all. But the narrative perspective has been abruptly and briefly projected to the watching heath creatures, and what they are seeing is described as a "performance" (161), one that intrigues and mystifies them, like an incomprehensible but fascinating ritual or game. This sense of the heath as a type of Eden derives, that is to say, from the superimposition of an "innocent" point of view on the scene of an unremarkable human routine.

Egdon not only ceases for the time being to be barren but even seems, in the heart of winter, to acquire an idyllic vernal promise. The motif of the paradisal so suddenly established at the beginning of Book Second hinges not just on an allusion to Adam, then, but also on a shift in perspective that transforms work into the kind of play suggested by the idea of performance. In Book First the word *performance* was used to characterize Eustacia's first appearance on Rainbarrow and, less appropriately, of Thomasin's initial behavior as interpreted by Mrs. Yeobright. In Book Second, *performance* in fact becomes a key word. Almost every event described in this book has something of the peculiarly ceremonious quality that so strikingly informs both Eustacia's dream and, in a different way, the enactment of the Saint George play.

Unlike the puzzled birds, reptiles, and rabbits, however, Eustacia does not actually witness Humphrey and Sam's performance; rather, their voices and words about Clym Yeobright come down the chimney to her as she sits in the dining room. The curious spatial relations between this aspect of the domestic interior of Mistover Knap and the world immediately outside it suggest again that Eustacia is somehow beneath the surface of the earth and that the workmen are above it. Or, perhaps more accurately, what they suggest is the notion that Eustacia is at the bottom of the sea:

> She entered the recess [of the chimney corner], and, listening, looked up the old irregular shaft, with its cavernous hollows, where the smoke blundered about on its way to the square bit of sky at the top, from which the daylight struck down with a pallid glare upon the tatters of soot draping the flue as seaweed drapes a rocky fissure. (161–62)

At any rate, whether the metaphorical context here is subterranean or submarine, Eustacia has no part in the idyllic scene outside or above: at this stage she is still aware of herself only as an exile, a woman banished from the world, as she imagines it, of fulfilled desire. But what Humphrey and Sam have to say about Clym inspires her now to make what she thinks of as a "pilgrimage" (165) to Blooms-End: "To look at the palings before the Yeobrights' house had the dignity of a necessary performance. Strange that such a piece of idling should have seemed an important errand" (165). And this, the first of several "performances" by Eustacia in Book Second, does, in a way, afford her a glimpse of paradise.

Her errand is important because the fence outside Blooms-End is almost literally the line that divides the barrenness of the heath from the more fertile world of nature beyond it. And it is the symbolic significance of this dividing line that gives Eustacia's "performance" its point:

> Beyond the irregular carpet of grass was a row of white palings, which marked the verge of the heath in this latitude. They showed upon the dusky scene that they bordered as distinctly as white lace

on velvet. Behind the white palings was a little garden; behind the
garden an old, irregular, thatched house, facing the heath. . . .
This was the obscure, removed spot to which was about to return
a man whose latter life had been passed in the French capital—the
centre and vortex of the fashionable world. (165)

From Eustacia's point of view, it is as if, again almost literally, she
stands outside a paradise from which she has always felt excluded, the
palings suggesting bars that shut her out from a place that she now sees
as the symbol of a more abundant kind of life. Her performance consists simply in the act of looking at or trying to see inside the palings,
for there seems nothing more she can do; and of course the scene
evokes the image of a banished Eve standing longingly outside the
locked gates of Eden after the fall.

We are immediately confronted with conspicuous yet paradoxical variations on the same motif when the narrative shifts to Thomasin
in Chapter 2. Thomasin's Christmas preparations at Blooms-End have
even more the air of "a necessary performance" than does Eustacia's
pilgrimage there. And in that these activities constitute a form of ceremonious work, they recall the scene witnessed by the heath creatures
at the outset. But they also differ from Humphrey and Sam's activity in
one crucial respect: the furze-stacking operation looked like a kind of
"pageantry" only in the sense that, to those watchers, its meaning
seemed obscure; Thomasin's actions amount to a performance precisely in the sense that their significance seems so iconographically transparent. She appears first as an abandoned and lonely woman against
the backdrop of a symbolic abundance of apples in the loft over her
aunt's fuel house. And as if to underline the fact that Thomasin, just as
much as Eustacia, finds herself in the role of the fallen Eve, she asks,
"Now, look at me as I kneel here, picking up these apples—do I look
like a lost woman? . . . I wish all good women were as good as I!"
(167). The parallel to the lost Eve is suggested even more pointedly
when she appears again, standing unhappily in the branches of the
holly tree. Thomasin's situation, in other words, echoes that of
Eustacia, so that the meaning of each of their respective performances
illuminates the other.

The odd thing about this reflection effect, of course, is that from Eustacia's point of view, Thomasin's situation appears to be so much more advantageous than her own: living in the same house as Clym, Thomasin is on the other side of the white palings. The palings are like prison bars for Eustacia, not just in the sense that they signify her exclusion from an imagined paradise but also because they seem to lock her in as well as out, confining her to the world of the heath. Yet Thomasin, too, is held captive by the white palings: in fact, until she finally leaves Blooms-End at the end of Book Second to marry Wildeve, she seems even more a prisoner there than Eustacia does outside. "Inside is Paradise," we are told, and one of the key visual paradigms in this book is that of the outsider looking longingly in; but inside and outside would seem in effect to be merely mirror images of each other, the distinction between them no more than an aspect of the illusion inherent in all visual perspective. There is nothing illusory, however, about what the distinction symbolizes—the hunger for meaning, for the kind of significant revelation that an "inside" world is assumed to be capable of affording.

Both the illusion and the hunger are simultaneously epitomized in Eustacia's dream. And the dream as yet another type of performance is at once transparent and opaque. On the one hand, it is an ordinary adolescent fantasy, a trivial wish-fulfillment dream featuring the idea of rescue by a knight in armor who is also the embodiment of an ideal of erotic liberation. On the other, though, it is curiously ritualized and mysteriously resonant: for the dreamer, it has the same quality of suggestive but not quite decipherable ceremoniousness that the initial furze-stacking episode seems to have had for the watching animals. Its initial "transformation scenes" (173) evoke the notion of the identity transfiguration that Eustacia anticipates from the experience of love, which she believes will precipitate her escape—for the dream "had as many ramifications as the Cretan labyrinth" (173)—from the confusions and frustrations of her heath-bound existence. In the dream's central episode, this rather sinister labyrinth image is itself transformed into the formal and benign "mazes" of an "ecstatic" dance (174); the transforming agent here is of course Eustacia's partner, "the man in silver armour who had accompanied her through the previous fantastic changes" (174). The visor of the knight's helmet, however, is closed, and although Eustacia already feels "like a woman in Paradise" (174), the revelation of *his* identity seems to be the dream's real goal.

While in one sense the rescuing knight is obviously Clym Yeobright, what this fact actually means for Eustacia is best understood in the light of a crucial event immediately preceding the dream—her first glimpse of Clym on the evening before. After "straining her eyes in the direction of Mrs Yeobright's house" (171), Eustacia had finally turned her back on the white palings and returned in the direction of Mistover Knap. Then, quite fortuitously, she had almost bumped into Clym himself as he returned to Blooms-End with his aunt and Thomasin. He had even wished her "Good night!" (171)—the "Little Sound" that "Produced A Great Dream" (171)—but in the dark she could not actually make out his features. In the dream, then, the knight's face is correspondingly concealed by his visor. But at the climactic moment, in which "she saw him removing his casque to kiss her . . . there was a cracking noise and his figure fell into fragments like a pack of cards" (174). Or, we might add, like a shattered mirror.

For the revelation of the faceless Clym in the dream is in fact a dark joke about projected self-reflection. He is an insubstantial, ghoulish apparition that modulates into a conventional image of fatality even as he is about to identify himself; he is a mocking demonic illusion, a lover who is actually a death figure. Even in the dream context he is unreal, and so, above all, he is the embodiment of Eustacia's narcissism. T. R. Wright has pointed out that Eustacia "falls in love with an image of Clym Yeobright fashioned more from her needs than from his qualities"[9] and the only tangible reality she has to work with at this stage is her experience of his face as something hidden from her. This image—Clym's entire imagined identity as amounting to a kind of ontological blankness or nullity—is in every sense her own.

From one point of view the dream's meaning is almost absurdly clear: promising a revelation that it fails to deliver, it suggests that all such dream visions of paradisal bliss are merely chimerical. At the same time, however, as T. R. Wright goes on to note: "It is an extraordinary dream, symbolising as it does the fall of man (and woman) as a result of desire, which cannot be satisfied since the image upon which it fixes fractures into fragments. What they are seeking remains unspecified, capturing the vagueness and fluidity of all dreams" (Wright, 60). To put it another way, Eustacia is unconsciously re-enacting her initial performance as a type of lost Eve, straining her eyes pointlessly before the palings that stand between the heath and the Blooms-End garden. For although the heath in the dream is itself apparently transformed into a paradise to which Eustacia seems at last to have been admitted, at the end she still finds herself "outside" rather than "inside" it: the white fence has simply been changed into the knight's silver visor.

Up to this point Eustacia's role has not been much less passive than Thomasin's. In matters of the heart, of course, a becoming shyness—the downcast eyes of the modest and sequestered maiden—is the conventionally appropriate attitude for young Victorian women. But Eustacia becomes increasingly fixated on the idea of actually *seeing* Clym: "If she had had a little less pride she might have gone and circumambulated the Yeobrights' premises at Blooms-End at any maidenly sacrifice until she had seen him" (174). Although she does not go quite as far as that, we are told that nevertheless she "kept her eyes employed" (174): she wanders the heath, looking for him, and on at least one occasion "she saw the white paling about half a mile off; but he did not appear" (175). At this stage "seeing" becomes in fact a kind of obsession in the text, almost a form of desire in its own right, the narrator even referring now to a general "appetite" among the heath dwellers "for seeing and being seen" (176). And now Eustacia virtually insists on being granted the revelation denied her in the dream. Unlike Thomasin, she rebels, covertly at least, against her constrained female state, deciding to bring the whole matter of seeing and being seen more directly under her own control and refusing simply to wait for Clym to reveal himself to her.

As she spies on the Saint George mummers while they rehearse, she conceives the scheme of getting inside the white palings at Blooms-End by insinuating herself secretly into the play—a "performance" (204), she not quite accurately tells her grandfather later, that "was my first . . . and . . . certainly will be my last" (204). In literally becoming a performer Eustacia takes on a decisively masculine role, and not just in the sense that she plays the part of a male character. She abandons passivity and waiting in favor of initiative and action. And the irony implicit in this symbolic switch of genders is of course compounded by the curiously feminized appearance of the other actors. The boys' costumes have been made by their sisters and sweethearts, who "could never be brought to respect tradition in designing and decorating the armour; they insisted on attaching loops and bows of silk and velvet in any situation pleasing to their taste" (178). This has the effect of compromising the traditionally martial appearance of the various knights:

> It might be that Joe, who fought on the side of Christendom, had a sweetheart, and that Jim, who fought on the side of the Moslem, had one likewise. During the making of the costumes it would come to the knowledge of Joe's sweetheart that Jim's was putting brilliant silk scallops at the bottom of her lover's surcoat, in addition to the ribbons of the visor, the bars of which, being invariably formed of coloured strips about half an inch wide hanging before the face, were mostly of that material. Joe's sweetheart straightway placed brilliant silk on the scallops of the hem in question, and, going a little further, added ribbon tufts to the shoulder pieces. Jim's, not to be outdone, would affix bows and rosettes everywhere. (179)

Although such a feminizing influence might easily be seen as laudable, it nevertheless has an odd and somewhat confusing impact on the actual performance of the play: "in the end the Valiant Soldier, of the Christian army, was distinguished by no peculiarity of accoutrement from the Turkish Knight; and what was worse, on a casual view Saint George himself might be mistaken for his deadly enemy, the Saracen" (179). There is a general blurring not only of sexual identity but of the basic roles of the characters themselves, with the effect seeming to be the reduction of the great struggle between Christian and infidel to a slightly ludicrous competition among women over "scraps of fluttering colour" (178). In mythic terms, in other words, this kind of departure from tradition tends to suggest a decline in virility, a ritualized loss of male vitality on Egdon Heath that finds more direct expression, as we have seen, in the fearfulness and ineffectuality of someone like Christian Cantle.

It is a tendency underscored by Eustacia's own attitude to the whole project of the Saint George play:

> For mummers and mumming Eustacia had the greatest contempt. The mummers themselves were not afflicted with any such feeling for their art, though at the same time they were not enthusiastic. A traditional pastime is to be distinguished from a mere revival in no more striking feature than in this, that while in the revival all is excitement and fervour, the survival is carried on with a stolidity and absence of stir which sets one wondering why a thing that is done so perfunctorily should be kept up at all. Like Balaam and other unwilling prophets, the agents seem moved by an inner compulsion to say and do their allotted parts whether they will or no. (178)

This woodenness that seems to inspire Eustacia's contempt has the effect as well of suggesting that the traditional performance has long since lost whatever original meaning it may have had for actors and audience alike. The polite response to the mumming is almost as automatic and mechanical as the players' acting. "This unweeting manner of performance," we are told, "is the true ring by which, in this refurbishing age, a fossilized survival may be known from a spurious reproduction" (178). The "survival" would seem to be the lesser of the two evils here; but the fact that it is perceived as "fossilized" heightens the effect of a diminished vitality, the sense that Egdon is indeed a wasteland virtually crying out for some agent of genuine revival, for a real as opposed to some "spurious" Saint George.

If Clym has been symbolically cast as such a figure, Eustacia casts herself, with an unconscious prophetic irony, as Saint George's mortal enemy. In taking on a male role, however, she also becomes a knight herself, so that it is her own face rather than his that is now concealed by the "bars" or hanging ribbons of a "visor." The situation in her dream, in other words, is closely echoed, yet, as J. B. Bullen points out,

> the terms of her dream are reversed. It is *she* who wears the visor, and it is *her* face that is obscured. With "the power of her face all lost" and "the charm of her emotions all disguised," the fascina-

tion of "her coquetry" is denied existence. At this point in the novel the face of Clym Yeobright moves into prominence, and it is his face which becomes a "spectacle" that both Eustacia and the reader are invited to observe.[10]

But before we do observe this spectacle—yet another kind of "performance"—we notice that the terms of the inside/outside dialectic would seem to have been reversed as well. The symmetry of the pattern is retained, but Eustacia now looks out from within. And as we might expect, the motif of sight becomes more obsessive than ever: this phase of the narrative turns, in fact, into a virtual orgy of seeing and being seen.

Becoming an actor gives Eustacia the "opportunity . . . of seeing the man whose influence was penetrating her like summer sun" (180), and as she walks with the other mummers to Blooms-End we are told that "She had come out to see a man who might possibly have the power to deliver her soul from a most deadly oppression. . . . Perhaps she would see a sufficient hero to-night" (187). She goes "through the gate in the white paling" (188) at last, so that she now stands in the garden outside the house itself: "Eustacia . . . had never seen the interior of this quaint old habitation" (188). At this stage, however, as the mummers are obliged to wait for the dancing inside to end, we realize that what all the emphasis on "seeing" means is that the barrier between "inside" and "outside" still stands. Even when Eustacia is eventually admitted to the house, we learn that because of "the confusing effect upon her vision of the ribboned visor which hid her features . . . she could faintly discern faces, and that was all" (191). The effect is both tantalizing and frustrating: no matter how close Eustacia gets to realizing her imagined vision of bliss, she is still in some sense excluded from it, still in the position of gazing longingly through the palings. And as the description of the fireplace settle confirms—"Outside . . . candles gutter, locks of hair wave, young women shiver, and old men sneeze. Inside is Paradise" (193)—even the homeliest of such visions keeps receding away from the observer to some new spatial interior.

When Clym's appearance is finally revealed, the visual motif and the inside/outside pattern continue to be closely linked to the motif of performance. His face constitutes a Rembrandt-like "spectacle" (194) to the watching Eustacia, because it is one in which "an inner strenuousness was preying upon an outer symmetry" (194), its superficial handsomeness compromised by the "parasite" of "thought" (194): "The face was well shaped, even excellently. But the mind within was beginning to use it as a mere waste tablet whereon to trace its idiosyncrasies as they developed themselves" (194). The picture does not conform to the type of the heroic man of action, and Eustacia is "troubled" (195); nevertheless, she has already fallen in love. She accepts a glass of wine from him, which "vanished inside the ribbons" (198) of her visor:

> At moments during this performance Eustacia was half in doubt about the security of her position; yet it had a fearful joy. A series of attentions paid to her, and yet not to her but to some imaginary person, by the first man she had ever been inclined to adore, complicated her emotions indescribably. She had loved him partly because he was exceptional in this scene, partly because she had determined to love him, chiefly because she was in desperate need of loving somebody after wearying of Wildeve. (198)

As her "fearful joy" suggests, she is also more than half in love with the "performance" itself, with concealment, indirection, and obliqueness. From Clym's perspective, as it must seem to Eustacia, it is she rather than he who is in effect inside the white palings now, "only the sparkle of her eyes being visible between the ribbons which covered her face" (198). Yet from her point of view, she remains an outsider, too. Thomasin appears in the pantry, "looking anxious, pale, and interesting . . . not well enough" (199–200) to join the party; but when Clym follows her "into the private room beyond" the door closes behind them, leaving Eustacia, who "saw and heard no more," in a state of "wild jealousy" (200). It is Thomasin in this perspective who remains the privileged insider.

Eustacia is by no means the only player in Book Second who is continually obliged in this way to take the part of the somewhat frustrated audience as well. Particularly in relation to Blooms-End, Diggory Venn always finds himself in much the same position. Owing to the combined machinations of Eustacia, Mrs. Yeobright, and Wildeve, for example, Diggory is briefly encouraged to renew his courtship of Thomasin. But even as he arrives at Blooms-End to press his suit, Thomasin's future is already in the process of being settled. He is left to stand at the gate to witness a performance that is described as if it were a kind of mime, the significance of which only gradually becomes apparent to the reader as well as to Diggory:

> He had reached the white palings and laid his hand upon the gate when the door of the house opened, and quickly closed again. A female form had glided in. At the same time a man, who had seemingly been standing with the woman in the porch, came forward from the house till he was face to face with Venn. (212)

From outside the fence Diggory watches a dramatic scene whose meaning remains obscure until the "man," finally identified as Wildeve, explains it to him, "I've claimed her and got her. Good night, reddleman!" (212). Diggory then goes up to the house and asks for Thomasin's aunt. But "instead of requesting him to enter she came to the porch" (212), and after only a brief conversation "Mrs Yeobright went in, and Venn sadly retraced his steps into the heath" (212). Diggory is not so much as invited inside the front door.

Eustacia, on the other hand, has not only managed to get inside Blooms-End but has succeeded in eliminating Thomasin as a rival for Clym's affection. Thomasin is figuratively cast out of the garden: she becomes "a little figure wending its way between the scratching furze-bushes, and diminishing far up the valley—a pale-blue spot in a vast field of neutral brown, solitary and undefended except by the power of her own hope" (217). Eustacia then quickly begins her preparations for taking over what she had regarded as Thomasin's cynosural female role. But even this role involves for Eustacia something of the same curious blurring of sexual identity that we saw in the Saint George play. She has not simply waited upon events, like Thomasin, but has actually taken a large part in instigating them and shaping their outcome—and she continues to do so. From being an aggrieved but passive woman trying forlornly to see *in*, she becomes an active and powerful figure, no longer quite visible herself, gazing triumphantly *out*. It is in this phase of the sequence of transformations in Book Second that Eustacia stages an astonishing dramatic scene of her own—her climactic performance in this section of the narrative and the visual finale of all its "pageantry" having to do with seeing and being seen.

We are told more than once that the wedding of Thomasin and Wildeve is to be "unceremonious" (214, 219). And so, as Diggory Venn describes it, it is—until Eustacia puts in her appearance. More than ever, she might now be thought of as a kind of female knight, for she shows up, uninvited but apparently out of disinterested courtesy, to offer the ritual service of giving away the bride. She is unrecognized at first, because her visor has now become a heavy veil. When she lifts it, the dramatic effect is considerable: we are told of Wildeve's "changing colour" (221) as she calmly tells him that "it gives me sincerest pleasure to see her your wife to-day" (222). Her victory is complete. Acting in the role traditionally assigned to the bride's father, Eustacia delivers her only rival into the hands of her no longer wanted former lover, thus disposing of both at once; this unmasking of her own identity becomes the final triumphant revelation in the whole visual dialectic of concealment and transparency, outwardness and inwardness, in terms of which so much of Book Second is constructed.

The episode also constitutes, of course, a grotesque mockery of the whole idea of "deliverance." Notwithstanding the element of spite, Eustacia's effrontery is impressive; but in relation to the structure of the myth to which the novel always alludes, her appropriation of a conventionally male role has a certain ominousness as well. If the world of the narrative up to this stage is characterized by the sense of an absence of male vitality—by dead fathers and by men generally perceived as weak or irresponsible—then the symbolism of Eustacia's actions at the wedding does little to improve matters. And she, as well as Thomasin, will marry the wrong man. The seasonal imagery in Book Second seems to point toward the type of climax that involves the revelation of a heroic redeemer; what we actually get, however—beyond the anticlimax of Clym's worried face—is yet another revelation of the woman who most longs for deliverance. Clym himself, hovering ineffectually in the background and only fretting from time to time about what he sees as the impropriety of Thomasin's behavior, has redeemed nothing so far. It is Eustacia, ironically, who usurps and hence parodies the heroic role: in this dramatic but vindictive unmasking that is also a brazen self-advertisement, almost a deliberate blazoning forth of her own beauty, it is as if she had decided to cast herself, rather than the knight of her dream, as the light of a new sun.

6

"The Fascination": Seeing Close

Why is it that a woman can see from a distance what a man cannot
see close?

As the Christmas performance of the Saint George play indicates, the
mythic context of the theme of deliverance in Book Second is primarily
Christian. I have already noted, however, Hardy's interest in conflating
Christian with other kinds of mythological symbolism, and this is
nowhere more evident than in the overall time scheme of *The Return
of the Native*. Beginning on 5 November and ending on 6 November,
the main action of the novel spans the course of a year and a day, so
that the narrative has a cyclical as well as a linear impetus, a structural
circularity that is clearly linked to the annual cycle of the seasons. In
Christian terms, the rhythm of the first three books involves an initial
sinking into winter's darkness and sterility, with, at its nadir, the coming of a hero whose presence seems to signal a reversal of the process,
followed by an emergence into the sunlight and fecundity of summer.
But the novel also incorporates an older form of this death-and-
resurrection sequence, a version of various ancient vegetation myths
in which the return of the crops every spring is ensured by the ritual

sacrifice every fall of a hero/victim who embodies the principle of fertility or life. The chief difference between the two stories is that while the structure of the older one suggests indefinite cyclical repetition, the Christian rhythm involves a climactic and conclusive dialectical thrust out of the darkness and into the light, out of the very circularity of the cycle itself.

In the novel as a whole, the older story is in fact primary. The motif of the annual sacrifice of an allotted victim is established at the beginning with the 5 November bonfires. For these represent not only the human assertion of life in the face of the onset of winter's darkness but also the ritual immolation of Guy Fawkes, the burning in effigy of that historical figure whose first name has actually come to connote the idea of the mocked and reviled scapegoat. This aspect of what the bonfires signify means that they also adumbrate the return of light in the spring—something that makes the allusions in Book Second to the coming of both Christ and Saint George seem either anomalous or superfluous, until we begin to see that Clym Yeobright's arrival is ironic rather than heroic. If anything, as the novel moves into its disastrous summer drought phase in Book Fourth, and as the darkness of November then approaches once again, what the shape of the narrative suggests is that Clym's real role is to be that of the next allotted victim.

But this view of Hardy's conflation of these two stories about death and rebirth is soon complicated by the realization that the similarities between them are at least as numerous and suggestive as the differences. Christ brings about new life by virtue of also being a sacrificial victim, and before he is resurrected he, too, descends into the world of death, although this occurs in the spring rather than in the fall and precedes his return to life by only three days. Similarly, Saint George is often pictured in traditional iconography as emerging in triumph from the jaws of a dragon by which he has first of all had to undergo the ordeal of being swallowed up: in effect, he rescues the maiden from the body or belly of death itself, and only after having himself been consumed. It is not surprising, then, that Book Third of *The Return of the Native,* which constitutes the spring and early summer phase of the cycle, tends to dramatize a curious tension between the motif of the renewal of life and the motif of sacrifice.

In the first place, the landscape of Egdon Heath is now radically transformed, its color changing from brown to green, its stillness giving way to animation. The narrative in Book Third returns again and again to the pond outside the bank at Mistover Knap, for this pool becomes not only the visual epitome of the transformation but also, almost literally, an image of living water:

> The month of March arrived, and the heath showed its first signs of awakening from winter trance. The awakening was almost feline in its stealthiness. The pool outside the bank by Eustacia's dwelling, which seemed as dead and desolate as ever to an observer who moved and made noises in his observation, would gradually disclose a state of great animation when silently watched awhile. A timid animal world had come to life for the season. Little tadpoles and efts began to bubble up through the water, and to race along beneath it; toads made noises like very young ducks, and advanced to the margin in twos and threes; overhead, bumble bees flew hither and thither in the thickening light, their drone coming and going like the sound of a gong. (249)

The process of natural regeneration is symbolically linked, of course, to Clym's desire both for Eustacia and for the awakening of Egdon's inhabitants from the intellectual and cultural equivalent of their own winter trance. The trouble is that Clym has a way of confusing these two different kinds of desire or, at best, of subordinating the first to the second. As Marlene Springer points out, he "is a victim of the fantasies of his idealism, and is thus blind to the basic human passions which govern the intended objects of his teaching: the heathmen, Eustacia, his mother, and even the simple Thomasin."[11]

But in terms of the principle of sympathetic magic that informs the myth of Saint George and the dragon, what the hero must ultimately bring to bear against sterility and death is his own vital energy, the basic human passion that is nothing less than his own virility. In this connection Mrs. Yeobright's first response to Clym's news that he plans to give up the diamond business in Paris and to become "a schoolmaster to the poor and ignorant" (233) on Egdon Heath has an ironic force that goes beyond her immediate disappointment and anger: "I have always supposed you were going to push straight on, as other men do—all who deserve the name—when they have been put in a good way of doing well" (233). She comes very close to impugning Clym's manliness here, and although she becomes resigned to his scheme in time, she never quite abandons this theme: "It is right that there should be schoolmasters, and missionaries, and all such men," she says, the words "all such" conveying a great deal, "[b]ut it is right, too, that I should try to lift you out of this life into something richer, and that you should not come back again, and be as if I had not tried at all" (236). Richer in this context is also more virile, and however crass such an identification might seem, the logic of the novel's symbolism tends to endorse it. From the psychoanalytic viewpoint, "doing well" means demonstrating sexual potency: as "filthy lucre," money signifies erotic power, and wealth is the pride of life itself. So diamonds represent the kind of buried or secret store of fabulous life that constitutes both the source and end of all human aspiration. In the world of sympathetic magic, treasure that comes from under the earth is always libidinal treasure.

In fairness to Clym, it needs to be said that he and his mother are not only at cross-purposes but arguing from dialectically opposed perspectives. Clym's dislike of his job in Paris had earlier been expressed to Timothy Fairway and the other rustics on the basis, precisely, that he found it *un*manly—"my business was the idlest, vainest, most effeminate business that ever a man could be put to" (229)—and he responds to Mrs. Yeobright's imputation by telling her in effect that she has got things backwards: "Mother, I hate the flashy business. Talk about men who deserve the name, can any man deserving the name waste his time in that effeminate way, when he sees half the world going to ruin for want of somebody to buckle to and teach them how to breast the misery they are born to?" (233). Clym's point of view— his hatred of luxury and ostentation, his sympathy with the poor and downtrodden—is an honorable one, with a moral substantiality that his mother's lacks. Still, Clym's view derives from a life-denying asceticism that bodes as ill for Eustacia Vye as it does for Mrs. Yeobright's hopes:

> there are many things other people care for which I don't; and that's partly why I think I ought to do this. For one thing, my body does not require much of me. I cannot enjoy delicacies; good things are wasted upon me. Well, I ought to turn that defect to advantage, and by being able to do without what other people require I can spend what such things cost upon anybody else. (234)

This is all very well, but it will not do for Eustacia; and when Clym goes on to invoke Saint Paul, the apostle of an asexual spirituality if not of outright sexual repression, we begin to detect an element of paradox in his conception of manliness—the sense that it is based on a distrust of phallic energy and a wish to sublimate physical appetite into something more exalted. Occasionally, we do get glimpses of a Clym who is not quite so alienated from his own body, as, for example, when his quarrel with his mother can sometimes be mysteriously healed by the currents of natural feeling between them: "He had despaired of reaching her by argument; and it was almost as a discovery to him that he could reach her by a magnetism which was as superior to words as words are to yells" (247). For the most part, however, his ascetic tendencies are given full rein, and not even his love for Eustacia does much to check them.

Though this asceticism looks at first like a rejection of nature itself, it in fact reflects a certain type of romantic nature worship, an affirmation of the pastoral ideal known as hard primitivism. Clym is always closely associated with the austere grandeur of Egdon Heath: "He was permeated with its scenes, with its substance, and with its odours. He might be said to be its product" (231). But the quality with which he actually identifies himself is the heath's aspect of uncompromising severity, the sense of the place as a dark and brooding anachronism:

> To many persons this Egdon was a place which had slipped out of its century generations ago, to intrude as an uncouth object into this. . . . How could this be otherwise in the days of square fields,

plashed hedges, and meadows watered on a plan so rectangular that on a fine day they look like silver gridirons? The farmer in his ride, who could smile at artificial grasses, look with solicitude at the coming corn, and sigh with sadness at the fly-eaten turnips, bestowed upon the distant upland of heath nothing better than a frown. But as for Yeobright, when he looked from the heights on his way he could not help indulging in a barbarous satisfaction at observing that, in some of the attempts at reclamation from the waste, tillage, after holding on for a year or two, had receded again in despair, the ferns and furze-tufts stubbornly reasserting themselves. (232)

What Clym likes best about the heath is the very fact that it cannot be cultivated, and his sense of affinity is not without a certain moral sublimity: it can be seen as an unconscious yearning for the natural condition of the lost garden of Eden. It can also, however, be seen as the willful embracing of a condition that in human terms amounts simply to desolation. Indeed, for all the lyrical accounts of the regeneration of nature in Book Third, Hardy constantly reminds us that Egdon is not to be envisioned as a blossoming meadow. One description of the heath, for instance, as Clym waits there for Eustacia on an early summer day, has a peculiarly sinister ring:

> He was in a nest of vivid green. The ferny vegetation round him, though so abundant, was quite uniform: it was a grove of machine-made foliage, a world of green triangles with saw-edges, and not a single flower. . . . The scene seemed to belong to the ancient world of the carboniferous period, when the forms of plants were few, and of the fern kind; when there was neither bud nor blossom, nothing but a monotonous extent of leafage, amid which no bird sang. (264)

The key words here are the adjectives—*uniform, machine-made, monotonous*—that can be read as foreshadowing something of the zombie-like automatism of the daily round of Clym's existence in the months ahead. Almost a science fiction wasteland, this is nature as an arena of sheer deathliness, and the allusion to Keats's "La Belle Dame Sans

Merci" in the final phrase attests to the nightmare side of the romantic dream of sublime nature.

In effect, then, Clym Yeobright sets about bringing new life to his people by virtue of a kind of deliberate self-mutilation, sacrificing what his mother would regard as his genuine vitality on the altar of an ascetic ideal of manhood. He is his own sacrificial victim, and the narrator tells us as much:

> Yeobright loved his kind. He had a conviction that the want of most men was knowledge of a sort which brings wisdom rather than affluence. He wished to raise the class at the expense of individuals rather than individuals at the expense of the class. What was more, he was ready at once to be the first unit sacrificed. (230)

We can infer from this that Clym's own ideal of manliness is peculiarly moralistic, in the sense that he perceives it as indistinguishable from such virtues as self-denial and stoicism in the face of hardship or difficulty. And although Clym is an extremist in this respect, as in others, such an ideal is not so far removed from the social norm in the world of this novel, as the ordinary texture of the lives of its inhabitants often tends to suggest.

The first episode in Book Third, for example, amounts to a kind of comical parody of this ideal. One Sunday morning the fact that Clym has not yet returned to Paris becomes the subject of a discussion at an open-air "hair-cutting" outside Timothy Fairway's house on the heath:

> These Sunday-morning hair-cuttings were performed by Fairway; the victim sitting on a chopping-block in front of the house, without a coat, and the neighbours gossiping around, idly observing the locks of hair as they rose upon the wind after the snip. . . . Summer and winter the scene was the same, unless the wind were more than usually blusterous, when the stool was shifted a few feet round the corner. To complain of cold in sitting out of doors, hatless and coatless, while Fairway told true stories between the cuts of the scissors, would have been to pronounce yourself no man at once. To flinch, exclaim, or move a muscle of the face at

the small stabs under the ear received from those instruments, or at scarifications of the neck by the comb, would have been thought a gross breach of good manners, considering that Fairway did it all for nothing. A bleeding about the poll on Sunday afternoons was amply accounted for by the explanation, "I have had my hair cut, you know." (227–28)

The scene not only parodies the strong-and-silent approach to the business of manliness but is ingeniously constructed as a description of a mock-heroic ritual sacrifice—almost, perhaps, as a mock fertility rite involving a displaced form of castration. When Clym joins the assembled heathmen to announce his intention of opening a school for them, it is as if the absurd note of sacrifice in the preceding account had ironically struck some responsive chord deep in his unconscious.

But while it is men who are perceived as symbolic victims in Book Third, it is the women who do the actual suffering. Thomasin is trapped in an increasingly unhappy marriage to Damon Wildeve. Mrs. Yeobright's misery over her son's abandonment of his affluent career is compounded by her grief and jealousy over his courtship of Eustacia Vye. And Eustacia, although she has fallen rather uneasily in love with Clym, receives not one but two wounds in the course of the events in this book, both of which are no less actual than symbolic: she is stabbed in the arm by the slightly deranged Susan Nunsuch, who believes her to be a witch, and soon afterward she is injured again, this time accidentally, at the hands of Clym himself. So the new career of the hero who is thought of as a deliverer—for all that it is based on a noble ideal of self-sacrifice—gets off to a dubious and ironic start. Far from being regenerative, the coming of Clym Yeobright seems to result in a general heightening of frustration and pain.

There is a striking contrast, in fact, between the lively transformation of the purely natural world in Book Third—the burgeoning of life on the heath itself—and what can be thought of as the corresponding sequence of changes in the distinctly human one. The terms of this contrast are specifically and somewhat curiously delineated at the outset in relation to yet another narratorial consideration of Clym Yeobright's face. At first this seems to be no more than an amplification of the meaning of the "spectacle" witnessed by Eustacia at the Christmas party in Book Second. Clym's is "the typical countenance of the future" because it bears marks "of mental concern" (225): "The view of life as a thing to be put up with, replacing that zest for existence which was so intense in early civilizations, must ultimately enter so thoroughly into the constitution of the advanced races that its facial expression will become accepted as a new artistic departure" (225). Clym's features express a visual conflict between the spontaneous and natural pride of life itself and the knowledge that life is more a burden than a blessing, an understanding that the human condition is at best ironic and at worst tragic: "That old-fashioned revelling in the general situation grows less and less possible as we uncover the defects of natural laws, and see the quandary that man is in by their operation" (225). In short, the life force exhibited in Clym is also subverted by his recognition that it lacks what in human terms would be a significant purpose.

At this stage the narrator suddenly shifts his figurative ground, moving from the imagery of the pictorial to that of the textual: "The observer's eye was arrested, not by his face as a picture, but by his face as a page; not by what it was, but by what it recorded. His features were attractive in the light of symbols, as sounds intrinsically common become attractive in language, and as shapes intrinsically simple become interesting in writing" (225). This shift is important, not only because it implies much about Clym himself but because it establishes one of the key motifs in Book Third, at the same time signaling a number of other crucial new developments as well. In this book we move from the world as performance or pageantry to the world as "text," from Eustacia's point of view to Clym's, from one way of seeing to another very different one.

If Eustacia is most clearly characterized by her hunger for life, Clym is best understood in terms of a type of withdrawal from it. In the beginning at least, there is nothing very unusual about this withdrawal: Clym is a bookish man, someone with a great deal of faith in the power of the printed page, and reading necessarily involves a temporary retreat from the direct experience of reality. It can also, of course, lead to withdrawal as a habit and, moreover, to the habit of seeing the world itself as a book, a text that constantly needs to be read and deciphered. Clym acquires both these habits, and his point of view, as distinct from Eustacia's, is summed up in two otherwise unrelated sentences in Book Third. During the episode in which the heathmen recover the bucket from the well at Mistover Knap, we are told that "Yeobright retired to the heap of recovered rope in a meditative mood" (241). At that moment he is trying, not inappropriately perhaps, to interpret Eustacia's cry of alarm when she saw that he was working without much concern for his safety. What is interesting here, however, is that his action is that of a man more accustomed, as "retired" and "meditative" suggest, to texts than to lost buckets or women's cries. A few weeks later his life seems to be utterly transformed by love: "When Yeobright was not with Eustacia he was sitting slavishly over his books; when he was not reading he was meeting her" (261). This sentence is constructed so as to make the two activities described in it seem almost interchangeable. In a way, for Clym, they are, but his reading of Eustacia could not be more wrong.

Clym, we learn, "was a John the Baptist who took ennoblement rather than repentance for his text" (230). Like his love for his "kind," what this suggests is an inclination to turn concrete experience into edifying abstractions. But while this abstracting tendency can be useful in the interpretation of written discourse, it has a distinctly blinkering effect on its practitioner when it is applied to the world of people and things. As Clym tells the rustics assembled at the Sunday morning haircutting about both the vanity of riches and his intention to improve their lives by educating them, our sense of his misguidedness derives not just from the disjunction between his earnestness and their subsequent skepticism but from the narrowness and obsessiveness of his vision. His scheme verges on absurdity precisely because it has so little genuine relevance to those lives. Abstractions like "ennoblement," in other words, seem to involve him in a kind of willful myopia, an inability to stand back and see the heath folk as they really are. If the world is like a book for Clym, the narrowness of his interpretive focus almost always causes him to misread it.

This effect is even more pronounced when he and Eustacia are alone together for the first time at Mistover Knap, an occasion that is in fact as densely charged with meaning as with feeling. Having finally managed to retrieve the bucket from the well only to find that its bottom has been "clean knocked out" (242), Fairway and the other men have gone home, leaving Eustacia murmuring "No water" (242), as if she were in the middle of a desert. Indeed, from her own point of view, that is precisely where she is: when Clym tells her that "there are no impurities in the water" (243) of the pool outside the bank, she responds haughtily, "I am managing to exist in a wilderness, but I cannot drink from a pond" (243). In the mythic context Clym's role is not simply to provide water but to renew for Eustacia the flow of nothing less than the water of life itself. He tries in effect to do so by lowering a pail into the wellspring; he succeeds only in leaving her holding a rope that tears the skin from the palm of her hand. This failure, however, has at least the positive result of bringing them physically closer together. She says that this "is the second time I have been wounded to-day" (244) and shows him the "bright red spot" on the "smooth surface" of "her round white arm," a mark "like a ruby on Parian marble" (244).

This scene is fraught with erotic intensity. The display of "wounds" is surely a text to which Clym should react appropriately, but, after deploring the superstitiousness of people like Eustacia's assailant, Susan Nunsuch, he merely says, "I have come to clean away these cobwebs. . . . Would you like to help me—by high class teaching? We might benefit them much" (244). Clym responds to the almost palpable eroticism of the moment by offering Eustacia a job. His misreading is absurdly reiterated soon afterward when he tells his mother, "She is excellently educated, and would make a good matron in a boarding-school" (251)—to which Mrs. Yeobright can only reply, "You are blinded, Clym" (252). Her choice of words is acute, not just in the sense that he is bedazzled but because the narrowness of his vision prevents him from seeing Eustacia any more clearly than he sees anyone else.

Because everything that he does must be invested with moral significance, Clym constantly turns his life into a certain type of narrative. The effect of their meeting at Mistover Knap is to create in Eustacia the sensation of a new emotional abundance: "She seemed full of many things. Her past was a blank, her life had begun" (245). As far as Clym is concerned, on the other hand, "his most intelligible sensation was that his scheme had somehow become glorified. A beautiful woman had been intertwined with it" (245). His reaction is also a kind of reading—a transformation of the moment of enchantment into an edifying text. As soon as he returns home he unpacks his books, arranges his desk, and says, "Now, I am ready to begin" (245). That evening, and all the next day, when he might perhaps have been expected to think about renewing his courtship, Clym spends reading.

The problem is not so much that of seeing the world as a text—most of the characters in the novel, and especially the men, see their world this way all the time—but with the particularly constricted terms in which Clym characteristically deciphers it. His tryst with Eustacia during a lunar eclipse, for instance, reveals once again his peculiar shortsightedness with respect to the situation's fairly conspicuous symbolic implications. As a central symbol of romance, the moon presides over the world of desire, and it is true enough that Clym regards the moon in this episode as a kind of distant reflection of his own romantic yearnings:

> More than ever he longed to be in some world where personal ambition was not the only recognized form of progress—such, perhaps, as might have been the case at some time or other in the silvery globe then shining upon him. His eye travelled over the length and breadth of that distant country—over the Bay of Rainbows, the sombre Sea of Crises, the Ocean of Storms, the Lake of Dreams, the vast Walled Plains, and the wondrous Ring Mountains—till he almost felt himself to be voyaging bodily through its wild scenes, standing on its hollow hills, traversing its deserts, descending its vales and old sea bottoms, or mounting to the edges of its craters. (254)

For Clym, the moon is emblematic not of love, primarily, but of his own rigorous social and moral ideals: its topography, as we gaze at it through his eyes, reminds us of nothing so much as the harsh and lonely austerity of Egdon Heath. Again, his reading is oddly out of tune with the sort of dreamily erotic mood that the scene evokes. And the same kind of incongruity attaches to the function of the eclipse as a prearranged "lover's signal" (254): "While he watched the far-removed landscape a tawny stain grew into being on the lower verge" (254). Besides suggesting a symbolic usurpation of the moon's nocturnal authority, inappropriate enough in the romantic circumstances here, this growing "stain" is highly ominous, foreshadowing the defilement of love. As a textual "signal" Clym might be expected to read more closely, the eclipse seems strikingly inauspicious, a particularly ill-chosen sign for his meeting with Eustacia. Yet he never notices this.

His figurative myopia soon causes Mrs. Yeobright to conclude bitterly, "Sons must be blind if they will. Why is it that a woman can see from a distance what a man cannot see close?" (273) Inspired by maternal jealousy, she is referring, of course, to Clym's inability to see Eustacia as she, Mrs. Yeobright, would wish him to; but the metaphorical terms in which she formulates her complaint have a larger resonance in the novel. Besides being an ironic prefiguring of the fact that Clym will quite literally be partially blind within a few months, her remark can be read almost as a kind of gloss on the effect of the narrative point of view in Book Third. Events in this phase of the story are seen chiefly through Clym's eyes, and when the narrative moves away from him, the perspective is still predominantly male. As far as Clym's mother is concerned, one of the characteristics of "a man's" point of view is shortsightedness—an incapacity to see "close," let alone "from a distance." If, for Clym, his experience is like a book, then he is a surprisingly poor reader—one who can draw any number of moral lessons from his texts while at the same time always missing the larger picture they convey. The shift from the pictorial motif of performance in Book Second to that of textuality in Book Third, in other words, is also a visual shift from the broad focus of the panoramic point of view, characterized by vividness and movement, to the narrow focus of what might be called the textualizing perspective, characterized by abstraction and withdrawal into a meditative stillness.

Although lacking Clym's concern with edification, most of the male characters in Book Third exhibit his inclination to turn reality into narrative. One of the subsidiary rituals at the Sunday morning hair-cuttings, for example, is the telling of "true stories" by Timothy

Fairway "between the cuts of the scissors" (227). And Clym and Mrs. Yeobright first hear the news about the pricking of Eustacia's arm in the same narrative form—a "story" (234) told not once but three times by, respectively, Christian, Humphrey, and Sam. Later, Damon Wildeve overcomes the last vestiges of Christian's reluctance to gamble for the Yeobright guineas by telling him a whole series of stories of the kind in which daring gamblers, although temporarily reduced to rags, end up by winning fabulous riches. While there is nothing particularly unusual about any of this, the comic undertones of the activity in each case tend to undermine the high seriousness of Clym's own earnest efforts at textualizing his world.

To turn experience into narrative in this way is to impose some sort of significance on that experience and, simultaneously, to give at least the illusion of having acquired some authority or control over it. So when Eustacia finally agrees to marry him, Clym's delight is at first unequivocal. What began as an educational "scheme" has in effect become a pastoral/moral romance; and, despite his growing quarrel with his mother, despite his faint and as yet barely acknowledged doubt about Eustacia's capacity to be the helpmate that he wants, he believes that this romance is soon to be actualized. At almost the next moment, however, his doubt suddenly becomes terribly tangible:

> Clym watched [Eustacia] as she retired towards the sun. The luminous rays wrapped her up with her increasing distance, and the rustle of her dress over the sprouting sedge and grass died away. As he watched, the dead flat of the scenery overpowered him, though he was fully alive to the beauty of that untarnished early summer green which was worn for the nonce by the poorest blade. There was something in its oppressive horizontality which too much reminded him of the arena of life; it gave him a sense of bare equality with, and no superiority to, a single living thing under the sun. (267)

Not only does Clym see Eustacia "from a distance" here, but the setting is now abruptly unfamiliar and alienating; it remains a kind of text, but not the one to which he has been accustomed. "Overpowered" and even diminished by the "oppressive horizontality," Clym has an intimation of his own impotence. It is as if his status has been reduced from omniscient author to that of helpless character—as if, in this sudden absence of all vertical dimension, of a "dead flat" into which the figure of Eustacia herself disappears, he has become merely an insignificant word written on an unintelligible page.

Clym's reading of his situation is for once perceptive, but even though something of his new sense of dread persists as his estrangement from his mother becomes complete, he forges ahead with his plans, and the wedding day arrives. Here the narrative shifts to Christian Cantle, Damon Wildeve, and Diggory Venn and the struggle, in the night gambling scene on the heath, for possession of the Yeobright guineas. Although Clym is no longer in the picture, however, his way of seeing is in fact dramatized more strikingly in this final episode than in any other in Book Third. The gambling scenes are characterized by an intense contraction of the players' visual focus. Both Christian and Wildeve, for example, "became so absorbed in the game that they took no heed of anything but the pigmy objects immediately beneath their eyes; the flat stone, the open lantern, the dice, and the few illuminated fern-leaves which lay under the light, were the whole world to them" (286). Later, though "[t]he light of the candle had . . . attracted heath-flies, moths, and other winged creatures of night, which floated round the lantern, flew into the flame, or beat about the faces" of Wildeve and Diggory Venn, "neither of the men paid much attention to these things, their eyes being concentrated upon the little flat stone, which to them was an arena vast and important as a battle-field" (290).

It is as if the players are readers and the dice are texts. The analogy is suggested quite explicitly after the lantern has been extinguished, when Wildeve collects the glow worms and arranges them in a circle on the stone: "It happened to be that season of the year at which glowworms put forth their greatest brilliancy, and the light they yielded was more than ample for the purpose, since it is possible on such nights to read the handwriting of a letter by the light of two or three" (293). We are perhaps meant to be reminded here, by a kind of parodic correspondence, of Clym straining his eyes nightly to read his books. At any rate, the dice certainly function as texts in the sense that the dots or "points . . . burnt upon each face with the end of a wire" (284) are signs that convey a great deal of meaning, depending on which two faces happen to be uppermost after every throw. For all that it is arbitrarily assigned, this significance is no less intense than the players' narrow and myopic visual focus and as completely detached from anything else in the scene. Like those in any text, the meanings of these signs are exclusively human constructs, relevant only to the world of distinctively human affairs.

So the gamblers behave as if the nonhuman realm—the world of the heath at night—had simply ceased to exist: "The incongruity between the men's deeds and their environment was great. Amid the soft juicy vegetation of the hollow in which they sat, the motionless and the uninhabited solitude, intruded the chink of guineas, the rattle of dice, the exclamations of the reckless players" (293). Yet this is only one aspect of the "incongruity." At other times the stillness of the players is contrasted with the insistent and intrusive animation of the nature that surrounds them—not just the "heath-flies, moths, and other winged creatures of night" that sometimes "beat about" their faces but also the eerie visitations of the wild heath-cropping ponies and ultimately, of course, of the large death's head moth that extinguishes their lantern. In fact, there is more here than merely an incongruity: it is as though a tiny arena of uniquely human significance were constantly in danger of being overwhelmed by the much vaster natural arena, as though indeed the heath were actually inclined to engulf both dice and men.

In the face of this obliterating tendency, however—in the heath's capacity to reduce human aspirations to insignificance—even Wildeve, who loses the second game, insists to the bitter end on the importance and meaningfulness of "the whole world" of "the little flat stone." One of the dice is swallowed up by the darkness when he throws them away in his anguish; the other splits in two after he has bitten it in a new fit of agitation, so that Diggory can only say of his own final throw, "I've thrown nothing at all" (294). Yet Wildeve's responding cry of defeat and despair—"Blank is less than one" (294)—also represents the absurd triumph of the perverser reaches of human ingenuity: between them, these two have succeeded in making a kind of authoritative text out of nothing more than a couple of unmarked fragments of wood.

In winning the hundred guineas that had been entrusted to Christian, Diggory manages to retrieve the Yeobright inheritance; because he does not know that half were meant for Clym, however, he gives them all to Thomasin. Clym is thus deprived not merely of a substantial sum of money but of a more important symbolic legacy. If, in the psychoanalytic perspective, money is libidinal energy, then these guineas that Clym's father intended to be handed on to him at his marriage amount to nothing less than the family's power of life, what might be called the continuity of the Yeobright potency. As Peter J. Casagrande puts it,

> the intense concern with the family guineas to be delivered to Clym at his wedding celebration may be a broadly humorous reference to the phrase the "family jewels," slang for a man's, particularly a husband's, testes, called jewels because they have inherent value as the source of new life and the guarantee of the family's future. This possibility is not contradicted by the fact that, after Christian loses the guineas to Wildeve, it is Wildeve and Diggory who vie for the guineas, just as they vie for the hand of Thomasin. It is in them, Thomasin's husbands, that the future of the Yeobrights lies. They, not Clym, who will lose Eustacia to Wildeve, and certainly not Christian, are the active, successful males in this veiled sexual combat. (Casagrande, 126–27)

It is Christian, however, who recognizes the peculiar authority of the dice themselves in this sexual combat, even if he sees them in a quasi-supernatural light:

> "What magical machines these little things be, Mr. Wildeve! 'Tis a game I should never get tired of. Would you mind my taking 'em out and looking at 'em for a minute, to see how they are made? I didn't like to look close before the other men, for fear they should think it bad manners in me." Christian took them out and examined them in the hollow of his hand by the lantern light. "That these little things should carry such luck, and such charm,

and such a spell, and such power in 'em, passes all I ever heard or zeed." (284)

And as Wildeve eggs him on—"You ought to win some money, now that you've got them. Any woman would marry you then" (284)—it becomes clear that for Christian the dice are the very symbols of the virility he has always lacked.

Not only do the dice "magically" contain or control the outcome of the game—possession of the guineas—but what happens to them foreshadows what happens to Clym. One die is lost and the other broken, and Clym becomes a man who seems somehow fundamentally crippled, who withdraws altogether from the arena of active life. With his readiness "to be the first unit sacrificed" in a scheme "to raise the class at the expense of individuals," he becomes in fact a victim of a type that his narrow rationalism and idealism can neither have anticipated nor allowed him to understand. Bewildered by Eustacia's dissatisfaction with their marriage and grieving over his estrangement from his mother, Clym will soon find himself more completely assimilated to the world of the heath and more helplessly lost there than he could ever have dreamed possible.

7

"The Closed Door": Earthbound in Eden

... a brown spot in the midst of an expanse of olive-green gorse

Despite all the unpromising signs, the marriage of Clym and Eustacia gets off to a remarkably idyllic start. Book Fourth begins in high summer, "the one season of the year . . . in which the heath was gorgeous"; and "in their little house at Alderworth" we find them "living on with a monotony which was delightful to them" (299):

> The heath and changes of weather were quite blotted out from their eyes for the present. They were enclosed in a sort of luminous mist, which hid from them surroundings of any inharmonious colour, and gave to all things the character of light. When it rained they were charmed, because they could remain indoors together all day with such a show of reason; when it was fine they were charmed, because they could sit together on the hills. They were like those double stars which revolve round and round each other, and from a distance appear to be one. (299)

Far from fulfilling the ill omens of Book Third, their idyll in this honeymoon phase of the marriage seems to substantiate the suggestion at the beginning of Book Second of Egdon as a kind of paradise. This state of affairs does not, of course, last long: while the "absolute solitude in which they lived intensified their reciprocal thoughts" (299), it also has "the disadvantage of consuming their mutual affections at a fearfully prodigal rate," so that Clym cannot avoid "the thought that the quality of finiteness was not foreign to Eden" (299). Their condition is paradisal, in other words, only so long as their sense of transcendent bliss can be experienced as something boundless and unconstrained.

Even for as long as it lasts, however, this happiness is never quite free from the mundane contingencies of ordinary existence. The "monotony" in which they live may be delightful, but it is still monotony, and Clym and Eustacia remain earthbound. Though the weather does not matter to them, this is nevertheless a paradise in which it sometimes rains, and where they are kept indoors. They may indeed be like "double stars," but only "from a distance" do they "appear to be one." Admittedly, their sense of transcendence here seems to be perfectly harmonized with the conditions of "finiteness." Nonetheless, their freedom is not absolute; always underlying it, paradoxically, is the element of constraint. And the harmony is soon to be disrupted. The discord that quickly develops between Eustacia and Clym begins with an inevitable conflict between the desire for transcendence on the one hand and, on the other, a capacity to accept the state of being earthbound, to put up with all the natural constraints of non-Edenic life. These become the antithetical terms, in fact, of a figurative dialectic on which the structure of Book Fourth can be seen to be based.

Transcendence is associated primarily with Eustacia and expressed most simply in her "dream" of having "the power of inducing [Clym] to return to Paris" (300). Paris in Eustacia's mind constitutes the ultimate paradisal place, its quasi-mythic status indicated by the way in which she thinks of its pleasures as limitless; she sees it as a place, unlike Egdon, where there would be no hindrance whatever to the complete fulfillment of desire. As we might expect, then, the imagery of transcendence in this Book tends to be that of escape, travel, flight, or of some imagined suspension of the law of gravity. Conversely, the idea of constraint, associated primarily with Clym, is expressed not only in terms of the normally austere reality of the heath but in imagery of immobilization, imprisonment, oppression, or of some form of increase in gravity's downward pull, an intensification of the earthbound character of human life. When Eustacia informs her new husband, for instance, that she has just quarreled bitterly with his mother, we are told that "A weight fell like a stone upon Clym" (306). When he first becomes partially blind, he is "shut up" (309) for a month in a darkened room. The effect of this confinement is to make the monotony at Alderworth suddenly seem less than delightful and to make Eustacia feel as if it is she who is the prisoner: "That dream of beautiful Paris was not likely to cohere into substance in the presence of this misfortune . . . her mind ran more and more in this mournful groove, and she would go away from him into the garden and weep despairing tears" (309). When Clym tells her that if he becomes a furze-cutter "we shall be fairly well off," she responds, "In comparison with slaves, and the Israelites in Egypt, and such people!" (311).

This dialectic of freedom and constraint is reflected in what has been called Hardy's "bifocal"[12] narrative perspective—the two quite distinct visual distances that I have noted from the outset in *The Return of the Native*. On the one hand, there is a resumption and indeed a heightening of the narrow, myopic effect that characterized the vision of the gamblers in Book Third. Paradoxically, the damage done to Clym's eyes by excessive study has led to a type of impairment that seems in practice to amount to an intensification of his habitual way of seeing. And, again paradoxically, this seems to restore him after his month of dark confinement to a solitary version of the paradisal idyll with which Book Fourth had begun. Cutting furze on the heath, he is perceived, from his own point of view, as a kind of innocent Adam in an unfallen Eden:

> His daily life was of a curious microscopic sort, his whole world being limited to a circuit of a few feet from his person. His familiars were creeping and winged things, and they seemed to enroll him in their band. Bees hummed around his ears with an intimate air, and tugged at the heath and furze-flowers at his side in such numbers as to weigh them down to the sod. The strange amber-

coloured butterflies which Egdon produced, and which were
never seen elsewhere, quivered in the breath of his lips, alighted
upon his bowed back, and sported with the glittering point of his
hook as he flourished it up and down. Tribes of emerald-green
grasshoppers leaped over his feet, falling awkwardly on their
backs, heads, or hips, like unskilful acrobats, as chance might rule;
or engaged themselves in noisy flirtations under the fern-fronds
with silent ones of homely hue. Huge flies, ignorant of larders and
wire-netting, and quite in a savage state, buzzed about him without knowing that he was a man. In and out of the fern-dells
snakes glided in their most brilliant blue and yellow guise, it being
the season immediately following the shedding of their old skins,
when their colours are brightest. Litters of young rabbits came out
from their forms to sun themselves upon hillocks, the hot beams
blazing through the delicate tissue of each thin-fleshed ear, and
firing it to a blood-red transparency in which the veins could be
seen. None of them feared him. (312)

The effect of Clym's affliction—the "curious microscopic" vision—has
been to reinforce his sense of affinity with the heath, to establish an
even closer intimacy between him and its natural inhabitants, and thus
to liberate him, at least for the time being, from the difficulties and
tensions in his human relationships. Within the constraints imposed on
him by his illness, he finds a new freedom.

Seen from a more distant viewpoint, on the other hand, his situation looks quite different:

This man from Paris was now so disguised by his leather accou-
trements, and by the goggles he was obliged to wear over his eyes,
that his closest friend might have passed by without recognizing
him. He was a brown spot in the midst of an expanse of olive-
green gorse, and nothing more. (312)

Clym has not only been more closely assimilated to the life of the
heath in this perspective; he has been virtually swallowed up by it. It is
as if not just his identity but his very humanity has been absorbed by
his surroundings, so that when Mrs. Yeobright sees him later, from the
same kind of distant vantage point, he appears to her "of a russet hue,

not more distinguishable from the scene around him than the green caterpillar from the leaf it feeds on" (338):

> The silent being who thus occupied himself seemed to be of no more account in life than an insect. He appeared as a mere parasite of the heath, fretting its surface in his daily labour as a moth frets a garment, entirely engrossed with its products, having no knowledge of anything in the world but fern, furze, heath, lichens, and moss. (339)

It is as if Clym has actually become one of the smaller heath creatures that do not fear him because they fail to recognize him as a man. In Eustacia's eyes, his manhood is significantly diminished by the nature of his new work. And, in almost literally being unable now to see beyond the end of his nose, Clym fails to discern how his occupation is likely to affect his marriage. For Eustacia, as for his mother, he appears to have been enslaved rather than liberated by the heath. His bondage takes the form already suggested by his objectification—what might be called an erosion of consciousness. We learn that the "monotony of his occupation soothed him, and was itself a pleasure" (313), but this soothing process is so hypnotic as to send him each afternoon into the kind of deep, heavy sleep from which even his mother's subsequent knocking at the door cannot awaken him.

The dialectic of bondage and liberation is reflected again in the changed circumstances of Eustacia's life and in her response to them. It is Eustacia's rather than Clym's sense of constraint that is apparent when he acknowledges that he is "a drag upon" her (318) and when she exclaims melodramatically that she will "shake . . . off" the "mockery of her hopes" (318) by going to the dance at East Egdon. This dance becomes the central emblem of transcendence in Book Fourth, and Eustacia's sense of at least temporary liberation seems to begin as soon as she sets out for it. Even in her appearance, as she leaves Alderworth, she seems to defy the principle of gravity: "The rebellious sadness that was rather too apparent when she sat indoors without a bonnet was cloaked and softened by her outdoor attire, which always had a sort of nebulousness about it, devoid of harsh edges anywhere;

so that her face looked out from its environment as from a cloud" (319). The effect is of Eustacia appearing almost to float above rather than merely walking along the first of the paths that will take her to East Egdon.

At this stage the imagery of paths, always a prominent feature of the novel's setting, begins to recur with a new insistence and resonance. For example, Diggory Venn will soon try to constrain Damon Wildeve from seeing Eustacia by setting a trap to ensnare him on the path that he habitually takes on his clandestine visits to Alderworth. Similarly, the narrator says of the dance at East Egdon that it "had come like an irresistible attack upon whatever sense of social order there was" in the minds of Eustacia and Wildeve, serving "to drive them back into old paths which were now doubly irregular" (324). The same metaphor is echoed later when Diggory tells Mrs. Yeobright about Clym's illness and advises her to visit Alderworth: "Your visits would make Wildeve walk straighter than he is inclined to do" (333). When Mrs. Yeobright does so, she nearly loses her way: "She tried one ascending path and another, and found that they led her astray" (338); on her return journey, the fact that "she had diverged from the straightest path homeward" and is "looking about to regain it" (348) causes her fateful meeting with little Johnny Nunsuch. Joseph Garver has pointed out that "the recurrent pattern of crossed paths" in the novel "graphically represents the characters' cross-purposes" (Garver, 90). More specifically, in fact, what this crisscrossing network of snaking paths suggests is the visual image of the maze, an archetypal symbol of confusion and bondage. Egdon Heath, seen from within its boundaries and from the "close-up" rather than the panoramic perspective, appears as a hellish labyrinth of intrigue and desire, frustration and betrayal, in which all the characters tend in one way or another to become lost.

Set against this image of constraint, yet also mimicking its structure, is the labyrinthine pattern of the country dance as a formal metaphor of transcendence. The dance is a maze from which the dancers already know their way out, so to speak, because they know its "figure" (322) or shape. J. Hillis Miller suggests that dancing in Hardy's novels is always a visual emblem of desire: "the circling dance of a group of lovers structures the dramatic action . . . as the characters revolve in complicated patterns of approach and withdrawal."[13] So, in *The Return of the Native,* the dance at East Egdon becomes the natural focus of Eustacia's longing for liberation—a transfigured version of her increasingly frustrated heathbound existence, a type of labyrinth in which she can achieve a joyful sense of release.

The governing dynamic in the lengthy account of this dance is the movement of flight. At first Eustacia stands alone and merely watches while the dancers "flew round and round" (320). Shortly after Wildeve has joined her, however, she pulls down her veil and quickly enters one of the outer "figures": "Fairly launched into the ceaseless glides and whirls which their new position as top couple opened up to them, Eustacia's pulses began to move too quickly for longer rumination of any kind" (322). And before long she "floated round and round on Wildeve's arm, her face rapt and statuesque; her soul had passed away from and forgotten her features, which were left empty and quiescent, as they always are when feeling goes beyond their register" (322–23). By the time she reaches the central "figure" Eustacia can no longer tell how much her ecstasy owes to the dance itself and how much to her partner:

> Wildeve by himself would have been merely an agitation; Wildeve added to the dance, and the moonlight, and the secrecy, began to be a delight. Whether his personality supplied the greater part of this sweetly compounded feeling, or whether the dance and the scene weighed the more therein, was a nice point upon which Eustacia herself was entirely in a cloud. (323)

Finally, it is as though she has transcended even the level of flight achieved by the rest of the dancers:

> Thus, for different reasons, what was to the rest an exhilarating movement was to these two a riding upon the whirlwind. . . . Through three dances in succession they spun their way; and then, fatigued with the incessant motion, Eustacia turned to quit the circle in which she had already remained too long. (323–24)

This episode echoes two related motifs from Book Second. In the first place, the dance seems to be the realization of Eustacia's prophetic dream, except that it is her own rather than her partner's face that is now concealed and that the partner is Wildeve rather than Clym. In a sense, though, the actual identity of her partner ultimately seems not much more significant in the dance than it had turned out to be in the dream: Eustacia's ecstasy is virtually self-generated and self-contained, and, as in the Saint George play, her own point of view is the only one that matters. As an extended metaphor of sexual performance, the account of the dance constitutes a small masterpiece of autoerotic fantasy. If the world is performance rather than text for Eustacia, it is she who is the leading actor. And, as in both the play and the wedding scene in Book Second, the veiled Eustacia finds herself in a dominant role, for whatever the conventions of the dance might be, the obsequious Wildeve is in every important sense the subservient partner. If Clym is unheroic as a leading actor, Eustacia now seems to take the heroic part.

The heroic is the central part, and the choreography of the dance involves a movement from a peripheral to a "central" figure (319), from an outer to an inner circle. So, in the second place, there is also an echo here of the outside/inside pattern from Book Second:

> How badly she had treated [Wildeve]! yet, here they were treading one measure. The enchantment of the dance surprised her. A clear line of difference divided like a tangible fence her experience within this maze of motion from her experience without it. Her beginning to dance had been like a change of atmosphere; outside, she had been steeped in arctic frigidity by comparison with the tropical sensations here. She had entered the dance from the troubled hours of her late life as one might enter a brilliant chamber after a night walk in a wood. (323)

The "tangible fence" reminds us of the white palings outside Blooms-End that had seemed both to imprison her on the heath and to exclude her from another imagined paradise. And the earlier motif is echoed even more explicitly in the movement from an outer darkness and coldness to an inner circle that is like a bright and "tropical" room.

One of the implications of this metaphor in relation to the dance, of course, is that Clym has been displaced by Eustacia's brief apotheosis, relegated now to the periphery of her life.

There is also something ominous, however, about Eustacia's moment of transcendence. Abruptly quitting "the circle in which she had already remained too long," even she seems to recognize that her centrality endangers her. The threat has to do only in part with the renewal of her dalliance with Wildeve, for the situation in the story as a whole—the increasingly destructive nature of the labyrinthine network of interdependent relationships—is perceptibly moving from pastoral romance to something much closer to tragedy. All the leading characters have in one way or another been victimized by Clym's marriage to Eustacia; the narrative's new direction seems to raise the question of which of these characters will qualify for the central tragic role. Clym's predilection for victimhood has long been apparent, and his crippling loss of sight suggests the possibility that he is destined to be not so much a type of Saint George as a tragic figure like the blinded Oedipus. The closeness of his attachment to his mother and the very depth of the breach between them do nothing to lessen the possibility. But at this juncture it is Mrs. Yeobright herself who suddenly appears to move toward the center of the tragic stage.

In the nearly infernal heat and aridity of the August drought, Egdon Heath becomes just such a stage, and the account of Mrs. Yeobright's journey across it alludes indirectly but unmistakably to the final ordeal of Shakespeare's King Lear. The focus of the narrative shifts once again from transcendence to constraint, from Eustacia's soaring flight at the dance to Mrs. Yeobright's sense of being weighed down on the heath. Ordinarily, we are told, she "would have found no inconvenience in walking to Alderworth, but the present torrid attack made the journey a heavy undertaking for a woman past middle age" (337). By the time she reaches the end of the third mile, even "the air around her" is "pulsating silently, and oppressing the earth with lassitude" (338). Nobody in the novel seems more earthbound than Mrs. Yeobright here, as she moves slowly and painfully toward her son's house. And the only other forms of natural life that the heath now appears to accommodate are virtually indistinguishable from the earth itself: "All the shallower ponds had decreased to a vaporous mud amid which the maggoty shapes of innumerable obscure creatures could be indistinctly seen, heaving and wallowing with enjoyment" (338).

By the time Mrs. Yeobright arrives at the clump of battered firs near Clym's house, she is not only oppressed but immobilized by the heat: "Here she sat for twenty minutes or more ere she could summon resolution to go down to the door, her courage being lowered to zero by her physical lassitude" (340). Although she does not know it, Clym lies unconscious in the house, but her own inertia seems in any case to be matched by the prostration of every visible kind of life. When she does finally come down the hill to the gate and looks into "the hot garden" (341) she sees

> the cat asleep on the bare gravel of the path, as if beds, rugs, and carpets were unendurable. The leaves of the hollyhocks hung like half-closed umbrellas, the sap almost simmered in the stems, and foliage with a smooth surface glared like metallic mirrors. A small apple tree . . . grew just inside the gate, the only one which throve in the garden . . . and among the fallen apples on the ground beneath were wasps rolling drunk with the juice, or creeping about the little caves in each fruit which they had eaten out before [being] stupefied by its sweetness. (341)

The apple tree reminds us that Alderworth is now a fallen paradise, though what this scene of stupefaction evokes even more strongly is the notion of a garden in hell. Because of its "perpetual moan," the clump of firs above the house is known as "the Devil's Bellows" (340): it is as if these trees were the very lungs of the heath and Mrs. Yeobright was no more than an obscure, ephemeral creature struggling in the vitals of a demonic earth-monster.

The subsequent sequence of events, in which Mrs. Yeobright is denied admission to the house, as she believes, by Clym, and in which Eustacia withdraws with Wildeve into an inner room, recapitulates once again the outside/inside pattern from Book Second. This time, however, the respective positions of the characters are reversed: it is Clym's mother who is excluded from this "paradise" and Eustacia who, only glancing briefly out the window, appears to exclude her. Other motifs and images from previous books are echoed and ironically parodied in much the same way as well. Water, for example, which had earlier been associated with the renewal of life, is either absent from Book Fourth (most of the heath pools having dried up in the heat) or present only as a destructive element. As the parched and exhausted Mrs. Yeobright creeps unsteadily back across the heath toward Blooms-End, she finds that the only pond-water available to her is unfit to drink: "it was so warm as to give her nausea, and she threw it away" (350). This scene of course echoes that in Book Third in which Eustacia scorns the idea of the pool outside Mistover Knap as a source of drinking water.

By this stage in the novel the element of fire has become destructive as well. The sun, for instance, has turned out to be not the source of revivifying warmth but merely a terrible furnace. It appears to Clym's mother, in fact, as a monstrous, life-devouring enemy: "The sun had now got far to the west of south and stood directly in her face, like some merciless incendiary, brand in hand, waiting to consume her" (351). Figuratively, the heath here seems not unlike the apocalyptic setting of the final section of T. S. Eliot's *The Waste Land;* even "the intermittent husky notes of the male grasshoppers" (351), which had appeared to be such innocent and playful creatures during the earlier account of Clym's furze-cutting, suggest the dry rasping mockery of the cicadas in Eliot's sterile landscape.

Just prior to Mrs. Yeobright's final collapse, there is also a recapitulation of the two distinct perspectives or ways of seeing in the novel and, correspondingly, of the dialectic of transcendence and constraint. The heartbroken woman sits down in "a little patch of shepherd's-thyme" that "intruded upon the path":

> In front of her a colony of ants had established a thoroughfare across the way, where they toiled a never-ending and heavy-laden throng. To look down upon them was like observing a city street from the top of a tower. She remembered that this bustle of ants had been in progress for years at the same spot—doubtless those

of the old times were the ancestors of these which walked there now. She leant back to obtain more thorough rest, and the soft eastern portion of the sky was as great a relief to her eyes as the thyme was to her head. While she looked a heron arose on that side of the sky and flew on with his face towards the sun. He had come dripping wet from some pool in the valleys, and as he flew the edges and lining of his wings, his thighs, and his breast were so caught up by the bright sunbeams that he appeared as if formed of burnished silver. Up in the zenith where he was seemed a free and happy place, away from all contact with the earthly ball to which she was pinioned; and she wished that she could arise uncrushed from its surface and fly as he flew then. (351)

This shift in vision—from the toiling, earthbound ants just beneath her eyes to the distant silvery heron in the sky—translates Mrs. Yeobright's grief into a longing for a release from bondage that is not so very different in kind from Eustacia's.

Even before she sees the heron, Mrs. Yeobright imagines her own almost "microscopic" view of the ants as what amounts to a bird's-eye view—as if she were "observing a city street from the top of a tower"— in an attempt to detach herself mentally from her sense of being "pinioned" and crushed. For the implied metaphor is of ant life as human life, the vision of "a never-ending and heavy-laden" toil reduced to insignificance by its perpetual and mindlessly mechanical repetitiveness, a continuous, apparently pointless reenactment of a genetic history whose meaning, if there is one, is impenetrable. It is precisely from this vision of despair that the flight of the heron seems to represent the possibility of liberation. But at the point of her own extinction, Mrs. Yeobright remains as earthbound as the ants, unable to distance herself or to break free of the natural bonds that have defined her life:

being a mother, it was inevitable that she should soon cease to ruminate upon her own condition. Had the track of her next thought been marked by a streak in the air, like the path of a meteor, it would have shown a direction contrary to the heron's, and have descended to the eastward upon the roof of Clym's house. (351–52)

The pathos of her situation finds another kind of expression in yet another dream. When Clym finally regains consciousness he tells Eustacia, "I dreamt that I took you to her house to make up differences, and when we got there we couldn't get in, though she kept on crying to us for help" (353). It is perhaps worthwhile to state the obvious here: that, unlike Eustacia's "dream" of Paris, Clym's is a dream of bondage. For in its ironic reversal of the situation that actually occurred while he was sleeping, what this dream confirms once again is that the condition of constraint has a natural and logical priority over that of transcendence, that no amount of journeying can release any of these three characters from an essentially immobilized isolation, that "inside" and "outside" are ultimately the same place. The "outcome" of the dream and the outcome of the situation that actually occurred amount to exactly the same thing. The horror of Mrs. Yeobright's end has a good deal to do with the fact that her last "thought" is also an unconscious acknowledgment that she is an ant rather than a heron.

Despite this, however, she is not, finally, without a certain transcendent dignity. If the heath has become in effect a desert by this stage of the story, one of the more curious minor ironies with respect to Mrs. Yeobright's final collapse is that it takes place in what looks like an oasis. The patch of thyme is a comparatively cool little green world in the midst of a hot expanse of sterile brown. So when we learn that she has been bitten in the foot by an adder, her death acquires a conspicuously mythic dimension. Snakes are not only the most earthbound of creatures but the symbolic embodiment of the bondage implicit in the "fallen" human condition. With his unfailing talent for a kind of terrified explicitness, Christian Cantle indicates the mythic significance of this adder bite as plainly as he can: "Neighbours, how do we know but that something of the old serpent in God's garden, that gied the apple to the young woman with no clothes, lives on in adders and snakes still?" (359). Book Fourth began with a paradisal love idyll; it ends with an allusion to the Edenic serpent. The effect is to give something of the resonance of an archetypal tragedy to Mrs. Yeobright's death.

The Return of the Native is the first of Hardy's great tragic novels, and in writing it he set out quite consciously to incorporate many of the elements of theatrical, and especially classical, tragedy. Joseph Warren Beach was one of the first critics to point out that the five books that comprise its main action correspond to the traditional five-act structure of the tragic drama, with the shorter sixth book constituting a kind of epilogue.[14] The novel observes the unities of place and time that shaped classical tragedy: the main action is confined entirely to Egdon Heath, and its temporal frame, though exceeding the limit of the single day prescribed by Aristotle, is pointedly restricted to a year and a day. I have noted the way in which Clym Yeobright's situation echoes that of Oedipus, and it is probably fair to say that Sophocles is Hardy's chief dramatic model. There are many allusions as well, of course, to the native English tradition of tragedy: besides the echoes of *King Lear*'s "blasted heath" in Book Fourth, for example, the confrontation scene in Eustacia's bedroom in Book Fifth is closely based, as Joseph Garver has demonstrated, on a scene from John Webster's Jacobean tragedy *The White Devil* (Garver, 115–16). The classical model, however, as represented by Aeschylus and Euripides as well as by Sophocles, does seem to be primary, even down to the way in which the heath-folk have the function of commenting on the main action like a traditional Greek chorus.

Classical tragedy for Hardy has an importance that goes beyond his modified observance of the traditional unities in *The Return of the Native*. This has to do with the Greek conception of the tragic hero, a figure typically characterized by a certain greatness or nobility of spirit whose downfall is inevitably brought about by a tragic flaw in personality—hubris or excessive pride. Reading Book Fourth of *The Return,* we can see how closely Clym Yeobright's character is designed to approximate that of the classical type without ever quite matching it. His initial, potentially heroic stature and nobility of mind have undergone a considerable diminution by now, and although he might be said to be afflicted with the sin of pride, this looks less like classical hubris than garden-variety stubbornness.

Similarly, while Mrs. Yeobright's death is profoundly tragic in the usual vernacular sense of that word, and even while the mythic associations of the adder bite give it a degree of tragic dignity, she does not quite seem to be the central figure in the thrust of the novel's now clearly tragic action. Mrs. Yeobright may sometimes appear as a Clytemnestra figure and is certainly proud, but her pride is no more the hubris of genuine tragedy than Clym's. Rather, it is essentially a blend of a snobbish sense of the local importance of her own family and a determination not to be seen to violate social convention. "Hubris," on the other hand, refers to the kind of Promethean pride that challenges nothing less than the authority of the gods themselves, that defies the constraints of circumstance and the dictates of fate. So the effect of little Johnny Nunsuch's announcement to Clym and the assembled heath-folk just after Mrs. Yeobright's death—"she was a broken-hearted woman and cast off by her son" (368)—is closer to the pathos of Victorian melodrama than to the pity and terror of true classical tragedy.

It is, of course, Eustacia Vye who is destined to play the part of tragic protagonist and victim. As soon as Clym begins to recede to nothing more than "a brown spot in the midst of an expanse of olive-green gorse," Eustacia moves to the foreground. That is clearly where she feels she belongs, but her aspiration has always been to become a romantic rather than a tragic heroine. Mrs. Yeobright's death, however, changes the picture altogether: it determines the nature of Eustacia's new role and can be seen as a prefiguring of her fate. The significance of the conflict between bondage and freedom in Book Fourth lies in the fact that it provides the context in which Eustacia must now operate. And for her, such a context is inevitably tragic. Unlike Clym and Mrs. Yeobright, or even Thomasin and Diggory Venn, Eustacia will not submit to the natural constraints that govern human existence. She will always demand a degree of transcendence that is impossible to achieve; in short, she will never acknowledge that she is an ant rather than a heron. The quality that had earlier seemed not much more than adolescent petulance is revealed in the new context as hubris. It is this quality that makes Eustacia such a potent central presence in the novel—she is a much more imposing and formidable figure than Clym—but it leads to her destruction as well.

8

"The Discovery": Speaking and Acting

It is with no strong desire, I assure you, that I play the part I have
lately played on earth.

As the narrative approaches its climax, the dialectic of constraint and
freedom, of bondage and transcendence, continues to be the informing structural principle. Book Fifth begins with the calm beauty of a
moonlight scene that is in conspicuous contrast to the inferno in
which Mrs. Yeobright had struggled and was consumed. But the "pale
lunar touches" that lend "divinity" (371) to Eustacia's face and seem
to make the landscape outside the Alderworth cottage shimmer in a
kind of sublime, transcendent peace are in fact deceptive. Eustacia is
leaning over the garden gate "as if to refresh herself awhile" (371),
which turns out to mean that she is escaping briefly from the situation
that faces her in the house. Inside Clym is once again confined to his
bed: "pale, haggard, wide awake, tossing to one side and the other, his
eyes lit by a hot light, as if the fire in their pupils were burning up their
substance" (371–72), he is locked in an inner turmoil of grief and
remorse. His situation echoes that of his confinement in Book Fourth,
but his struggle is now considerably more desperate. At the same time,

Eustacia's own sense of constraint as well as her desire to break free of it have intensified as well. And it is at this stage that a significant new element is added to the dialectic.

Perhaps the most striking feature of Clym's agitation is the extremity of the language with which he expresses it. When Eustacia comes in to tell him that "[t]he moon is shining beautifully, and there is not a leaf stirring," he replies, "What's the moon to a man like me? Let it shine—let anything be, so that I never see another day!" (372). He calls on God to kill him, crying, "I committed the guilt; and may the whole burden be on my head!" (373). The narrator tells us that "[d]uring his illness he had been continually talking thus," that "he longed for death as a field labourer longs for the shade" (372). It seems to Clym now that he is confined not by illness but by life itself, an imprisonment from which only death can release him—and he says so repeatedly. Language is important to this phase of his despair in another sense as well. "You had better not talk any more now," Eustacia says "faintly" (376), but the fact is that speech also provides him with some measure of relief:

> it was better for Yeobright himself when he spoke openly of his sharp regret, for in silence he endured infinitely more, and would sometimes remain so long in a tense, brooding mood, consuming himself by the gnawing of his thought, that it was imperatively necessary to make him talk aloud, that his grief might in some degree expend itself in the effort. (374)

The psychological paradox referred to here is familiar enough: his ravings constitute an emotional outlet, a means of release from the very torment that generates them.

Eustacia, on the other hand, has no such means of release. For reasons that are all too clear to the reader, if not yet to Clym, Eustacia is unable to speak freely, and her sense of verbal as well as physical constraint becomes no less dramatically palpable in this episode than the violence of Clym's words. When Humphrey comes to inquire after her husband's health, Eustacia makes "no reply beyond that of a slight catch in her breath, as of one who fain would speak but could not"

(371). On one occasion she responds to Clym's cries of anguish only with "one of those shivering sighs which used to shake her like a pestilent blast. She had not yet told" (372). On another "though her pale face remained calm, [she] writhed in her chair" (375).

Eustacia's silences are as meaningful as Clym's outbursts, and while her misery does not match his, the horror of her situation is distinguished by its peculiarly stifled, claustrophobic quality. She is "seared inwardly by a secret she dared not tell" (373). Sometimes "[t]he pallid Eustacia said nothing" (375) and at other times "declared that she could not give an opinion" (373). When Clym urges her to speak—"It would be better for you, Eustacia, if I were to die?"—her response is merely the ambiguity of "Don't press such a question" (376). To Wildeve, she whispers "I have not yet told him" (377), then bursts into tears:

> I—I can't tell you how unhappy I am! I can hardly bear this. I can tell nobody of my trouble—nobody knows of it but you. . . . I don't know what to do. Should I tell him or should I not tell him? I am always asking myself that. O, I want to tell him; and yet I am afraid. (377)

If speech offers Clym a means of release, Eustacia's sense of bondage is considerably worsened by this inability to "tell."

In any case, of course, language is for Clym the most natural mode of expression and communication. I have already noted his tendency to see the world as a text, whereas for Eustacia it is more like an arena of dramatic action or performance. And Clym actually seems aware of how he differs from his wife in this respect; for, later, when he has written asking her to return after she has left him, he only half-expects her reply to be in the form of a letter: "secretly Clym had a more pleasing hope. Eustacia might possibly decline to use her pen—it was rather her way to work silently—and surprise him by appearing at his door" (424). At this early stage, however, before her own secret has been revealed, no such significant gesture seems available to her. She must be silent, but at the same time there is apparently no meaningful action that she can perform.

Eustacia'a inability to "tell" appears to be almost infectious at first. When Clym recovers enough strength to walk about in the garden, even he lapses for a time into an uncharacteristic muteness:

> He was now unnaturally silent upon all of the past that related to his mother; and though Eustacia knew that he was thinking of it none the less, she was only too glad to escape the topic ever to bring it up anew. When his mind had been weaker his heart had led him to speak out; but reason having now somewhat recovered itself he sank into taciturnity. (379)

We soon learn, though, that not only is Clym still brooding over his mother's death, but that the evidently pointless horror of that death has in fact reinforced his habit of textualizing his world. "Meaning," in the sense of something to be deciphered from more or less obscure signs and signals, becomes no less a key word in Book Fifth than it was in Book First. In effect, as Clym grows calmer and sets about trying to learn what Mrs. Yeobright was doing on the heath on that August afternoon, his model becomes the mystery story: searching for witnesses and interpreting evidence, he adopts the conventionally literary posture of reader/detective.

Although he lacks the detachment conventionally implicit in such a posture, Clym is nevertheless quickly obsessed with what seems to be the ever-deepening "mystery" (384) that his mother's death represents. He asks Christian Cantle if he had seen Mrs. Yeobright on the day before she died; on being told that Christian actually saw her on the morning of the fateful day itself, "Clym's look lighted up. 'That's nearer still to my meaning'" (380), he exclaims. After questioning Diggory Venn and discovering his mother's declared intention to visit Alderworth, "Clym . . . passed from the dulness of sorrow to the fluctuation of carking incertitude" (384). Baffled, he decides at last to interrogate Johnny Nunsuch, for "when every obvious channel is blocked we grope towards the small and obscure. There was nothing else left to do; after that he would allow the enigma to drop into the abyss of undiscoverable things" (384–85).

When Johnny describes the events he had witnessed that hot afternoon outside the Alderworth cottage, however, Susan Nunsuch says, "Isn't there meaning in it?" (387). Clym echoes her—"Door kept shut, did you say? Kept shut, she looking out of window? Good heart of God!—what does it mean?" (387). By now, of course, his final question here has become rhetorical: the enigma has in one sense been all too clearly resolved. Clym's interrogations allow him to piece together a narrative that makes the circumstances leading up to Mrs. Yeobright's collapse intelligible in terms at least of their logic and sequence. In the moral sense, however, the abyss of undiscoverable things has actually deepened for Clym, and the mystery has become very much darker. The meaning of Eustacia's actions suggested by this narrative seems in an instant to transform Clym's universe into a nightmarish moral void.

The confrontation scene in Chapter 3 is based almost entirely on the tension generated by the conflict between Clym's need for words and Eustacia's determination to avoid them. When he returns home, Clym finds her standing before a mirror:

> She was not a woman given to speaking first at a meeting, and she allowed Clym to walk across in silence, without turning her head. He came behind her, and she saw his face in the glass. It was ashy, haggard, and terrible. Instead of starting towards him in sorrowful surprise, as even Eustacia, undemonstrative wife as she was, would have done in days before she burdened herself with a secret, she remained motionless, looking at him in the glass. And while she looked the carmine flush with which warmth and sound sleep had suffused her cheeks and neck, dissolved from view, and the death-like pallor in his face flew across into hers. He was close enough to see this, and the sight instigated his tongue. (389–90)

He tells her that she already knows "what is the matter," but "[s]he made no reply" (390). "Speak to me" (390), he insists, and his manner becomes physically threatening: "'Tell me the particulars of—my mother's death,' he said in a hard, panting whisper; 'or—I'll—I'll—'" (391). Frightened and playing for time, Eustacia seems at first to be ready to comply: "before you strike me listen. You will get nothing from me by a blow, even though it should kill me. . . . But perhaps you do not wish me to speak—killing may be all you mean?" (391). When he tells her, "I did think of it; but—I shall not" (391), she replies, "I almost wish you would kill me. . . . It is with no strong desire, I assure you, that I play the part I have lately played on earth. You are no blessing, my husband" (391).

If for Clym meaning pertains primarily to words, for Eustacia it has to do with some kind of performance—ideally a "part" she can act out with "strong desire." Both the sense of constraint and the need to escape are all on Eustacia's side now, but again there seems to be no significant action she can take that might release her. Clym, on the other hand, is in effect writing the climactic scene in the narrative that he has (re)constructed: his need is for some principle of satisfactory closure, and, like many a fictional detective, he seeks this by demanding a confession, an admission of guilt that will somehow restore moral coherence to his world. "The inhumanity," he thunders, "—I will not touch you—stand away from me—and confess every word!" (392). For Eustacia, however, the resolve to maintain her silence becomes in itself the sole minimal gesture she can make in the direction of asserting her freedom. "Never!" she replies; "I'll hold my tongue like the very death that I don't mind meeting, even though I can clear myself of half [of what] you believe by speaking. . . . Who of any dignity would take the trouble to clear cobwebs from a wild man's mind after such language as this?" (392).

Language continues to be a crucial issue as the scene proceeds. "Now, then, madam," says Clym, "tell me his name!" (392), and the next thought that occurs to him is of discovering proof of Eustacia's guilt in the form of a definitive text: "How often does he write to you? Where does he put his letters—when does he meet you? Ah, his letters!" (392). In order to find these, he overturns her desk, but "[b]y no stretch of meaning could any but a harmless construction be placed upon a single one of the letters themselves. The solitary exception was an empty envelope directed to her, and the handwriting was Wildeve's" (392). Unable to identify this handwriting, however, Clym can only bluster, while Eustacia remains "doggedly silent" (392), "Can you read, madam? Look at this envelope. Doubtless we shall find more soon, and what was inside them. . . . Do you brave me? do you stand me out, mistress? Answer . . . you refuse to answer?" (393). She does in fact answer, but not in the way that he wants: "I wouldn't tell you after this, if I were as innocent as the sweetest babe in heaven!" (393). Clym then resorts to a tactic in the literary rhetoric of interrogation familiar to any reader of detective stories: "Instead of hating you I could, I think, mourn for and pity you, if you were contrite, and would confess all" (393). Indeed, it is as if he were actually disclosing the specific type of fictional context within which he is operating: "Lost your voice, have you? It is natural after detection of that most noble trick" (394).

Eustacia's only response to all this is to tell him that she is leaving him. Her speech to that effect has two main themes: it is about a story without an ending—one that would therefore be pointless to tell—and also about the general inadequacy of words themselves:

> "You exaggerate fearfully," she said in a faint, weary voice; "but I cannot enter into my defence—it is not worth doing. You are nothing to me in future, and the past side of the story may as well remain untold. . . . Is this your cherishing—to put me into a hut like this, and keep me like the wife of a hind? You deceived me— not by words, but by appearances, which are less seen through than words. But the place will serve as well as any other—as somewhere to pass from—into my grave." Her words were smothered in her throat, and her head drooped down. (394)

In arguing that appearances are harder to see through than words, Eustacia maintains that a "lying" or inauthentic performance is worse than lying speech, that words are in effect less morally consequential than deeds. With respect to "meaning," the two of them are at something very like cross-purposes here. Clym nevertheless insists on hearing a confession from her, and, apparently overwhelmed at last, she seems finally to give him one:

> O, O! God have mercy upon a miserable woman! . . . You have beaten me in this game—I beg you to stay your hand in pity! . . . I confess that I—wilfully did not undo the door the first time she

knocked—but—I—should have unfastened it the second—if I had not thought you had gone to do it yourself. When I found you had not I opened it, but she was gone. (395)

In fact, Eustacia's familiarity with the strategies of rhetoric matches Clym's own: her confession amounts to a refusal to tell him anything more than he already knows. When he presses her to reveal what he really wants—the name of the man who had been in the cottage with her—she will not do so: "'I cannot tell,' she said desperately through her sobbing. 'Don't insist further—I cannot tell'" (395). Eustacia now performs the only action that, from her own point of view, still seems to be available to her: she leaves. Thus, with a conclusive dramatic gesture, she preempts the kind of detective-story closure to the story of Mrs. Yeobright's death that Clym has been trying so hard to realize. And even now, Hardy is at considerable pains to press home the point that language has indeed been at the heart of this bitter clash between them. After she has gone, Clym's obsession with the significance of words, with the importance of naming as opposed to performing, is underlined in his reaction to the news that Thomasin's child has just been born. "What a mockery!" he exclaims, on hearing that the baby is to be called Eustacia Clementine: "This unhappy marriage of mine to be perpetuated in that child's name!" (396).

If Clym's way of responding to his experience tends to be essentially literary, Eustacia's instincts are those of an actress. But leaving her husband does not in itself provide her with any clear-cut role: her "journey was at first as vague in direction as that of thistledown on the wind. She did not know what to do" (397). Eustacia needs to be able to perform, to "do," to find some mode of action that will answer to her situation. In effect, the situation now is that she is back where she started, and by the time she returns to her grandfather's house, her need for release seems more urgent than ever. Without even being aware that her young admirer, Charley, has become a spellbound one-man audience, she enacts the part of distraught captive: "Eustacia's face was not visible to Charley as she stood at the doorway, her back being to the sky, and the stable but indifferently lighted; but the wildness of her manner arrested his attention" (397). Instinctively, she "frames" herself here in such a way that Charley's response is to a considerable extent an aesthetic one. "[H]e had hardly deemed her a woman, wingless and earthly, subject to household conditions and domestic jars," so that, a little later, the "sight of her leaning like a helpless, despairing creature against a wild wet bank, filled him with an amazed horror" (398). Charley is like a spectator at a play, and his function in this respect is crucial.

It is not that Eustacia's actions are to be regarded as insincere or contrived, but that she is aesthetically distanced, as if she had been transformed into a performer on a stage, by the very starstruck quality of Charley's gaze. Even when, like Clym, she too behaves as if reality were a kind of text, our attention is drawn to the element of performance in such behavior, to the action of seeing things in that way as, in itself, a dramatic gesture. After noticing Captain Vye's brace of pistols, for example, "Eustacia regarded them long, as if they were the page of a book in which she read a new and strange matter. Quickly, like one afraid of herself, she returned downstairs and stood in deep thought" (400). The point here about her idea of suicide is that it is made visible. Together with Charley, we watch the notion becoming a definite purpose, as if Eustacia has at last found the part that she really wants to play: "The idea seemed to gather force within her, and she remained in a fixed attitude nearly ten minutes, when a certain finality was expressed in her gaze, and no longer the blankness of indecision" (400).

Almost everything here is conveyed by attitude and expression, so that when she goes back upstairs, only to find that the pistols have gone, Charley can tell her that he saw her "looking at them too long" (400): "I could not bear to leave them in your way. There was meaning in your look at them" (401). Indeed, the association of meaning with "looks" rather than with language is one that almost seems to run in the Vye family. When her grandfather comes home, he is "about to question her categorically; but on looking at her he withheld his words. 'Yes, it is too bad to talk of,'" Eustacia says "in answer to his glance." By way of response, "[h]e did not ask what it all meant, or why she had left her husband, but ordered the room to be prepared" (401).

Unable at least for the time being, then, to play a more active part, she can only revert to the role of captive. "A week passed," we are told, with "Eustacia never going out of the house" (402). But even when she does go out her sense of confinement makes the heath more like a prison than ever. What persuades us of this is the quality of suppression that now characterizes the restlessness of her movements— the sense that the constant constraint under which she had operated in the small Alderworth cottage has somehow simply been transferred to a larger and quieter setting. The critical fact is that Eustacia, more than ever, does not "know what to do"; she needs some form of significant action, but she lives in an enforced passivity. So when 5 November comes around again, and she sees Charley making a bonfire to cheer her up, she suddenly sees a possible means of liberation as well: "there flashed upon her imagination some other form which that fire might call up" (404).

Fire had been an agent of destruction in Book Fourth; to Eustacia, here, it seems once more to represent the chance of deliverance and renewal. The trouble is, of course, that she does not actually love the man who answers its apparent summons. Wildeve is rich now, however, and thus embodies the kind of potency that Clym so notably lacks. It is within his power, ironically, to offer Eustacia the abundant life she longs for. In fact, he offers her "anything" (407), including, specifically, the one thing that she wants more than any other—"to escape the place altogether" (407). She agrees to let him assist her "[i]n getting away from here" (407), but when he asks if he might go with her, "[s]he was silent." He repeats his request, but "[s]he was silent still" (407). What this constraint suggests is not just that she does not love Wildeve, or that she thinks him unworthy of her, but that the initiative for the act of leaving Egdon must be seen to be her own. The motivation for this particular performance must be clear, having to do only with her own "strong desire" and uncompromised by anyone else's. What Eustacia needs by this stage, in fact, is no longer a husband or even a lover but an autonomous power of action.

Nevertheless, uneasy though she is about Wildeve's role, she is also much revived for a time by the renewed scope for meaningful activity that her plan to escape provides. The act of lighting a fire above the bank at Mistover will become a more important gesture than it had ever been, a signal with a dramatic value far exceeding that of the mere words with which she explains its significance to Wildeve: some evening at eight, she tells him, such a fire "will mean that you are to be ready with a horse and trap at twelve o' clock the same night to drive me to Budmouth harbour in time for the morning boat" (408). Eustacia seems to be liberated now by the way in which, more than anything else, the details of her plan allow her to indulge her instinct for theatricality. By way of contrast, we learn that although Clym has in the meantime begun to have second thoughts and is busily revising his narrative construction of recent events, his own instinct for textualizing those events remains undiminished:

> Now that the first flush of his anger had paled he was disinclined to ascribe to her more than an indiscreet friendship with Wildeve, for there had not appeared in her manner the signs of dishonour. And this once admitted, an absolutely dark interpretation of her act towards his mother was no longer forced upon him. (410)

There is something faintly absurd about this ascribing and interpreting and close rereading of signs. Compared with Eustacia's renewed flair for the dramatic, Clym's conception of meaning seems slightly pedantic and almost irrelevant.

This conception is made less relevant still by the increasing urgency of Eustacia's desire for "flight" (416). Soon, we are told, "[e]ven the receipt of Clym's letter would not have stopped her" (419). Her conviction that she is effectively a prisoner becomes an obsession, and her movements resemble those of an animal pacing in a cage: "Eustacia could not rest indoors, having nothing more to do, and she wandered to and fro on the hill, not far from the house she was soon to leave" (416). The enlargement of her scope for movement actually seems to intensify her sense of bondage—a fact that, as she becomes aware of it, begins to look very ominous indeed: "She had used to think of the heath alone as an uncongenial spot to be in; she felt it now of the whole world" (416). But if the whole world is a prison, then flight itself is hopeless.

By the time Eustacia sets out on what will be her last journey, this ominous note has become all-pervasive. Nature itself seems "clothed in crape" and the night is "funereal" (419)—a night evoking all the "nocturnal scenes of disaster in the chronicles of the world" (420). This is the very archetype, in fact, of every fictive dark and stormy night. So the archetypal significance of the heath—an identification toward which all the novel's allusions to the Saint George legend have been pointing—suddenly comes into intensely sharp focus: "Skirting the pool she followed the path towards Rainbarrow, occasionally stumbling over twisted furze-roots, tufts of rushes, or oozing lumps of fleshy fungi, which at this season lay scattered about the heath like the rotten liver and lungs of some colossal animal" (420). This season, also the season in which the action of the novel began, reveals with abrupt clarity that the earlier manifestations of the heath as a paradisal place had been mere illusions, for Mrs. Yeobright's inferno and now Eustacia's place of captivity are ultimately revealed as the belly of a dragon, the monstrous embodiment of all the forces of deathliness that have been at work from the novel's outset.

As hero, Clym has been unable to see, let alone to slay, this "colossal animal," not because of his myopia but because he is in a sense part of the beast: together with everyone else, in effect, he has been trapped inside it all along. So when "Eustacia at length reached Rainbarrow, and stood still there to think" (420), we learn that her previous antipathy to the heath has by now become a dreadful affinity: "Never was harmony more perfect than that between the chaos of her mind and the chaos of the world without" (420). This is of course the demonic version of the idyllic harmony between mind and nature that we saw at the beginning of Book Fourth. By the end of the novel, as Rosemary Sumner has pointed out, Eustacia's "identity seems assimilated into the storm-swept heath and her death inevitable."[15] Her identity seems assimilated in this way precisely because the heath is in the process, figuratively speaking, of devouring her.

Now it is as if Eustacia had actually begun to sink into a kind of quagmire. Although water rather than fire is the chief destructive element here, her ordeal echoes that of Mrs. Yeobright in the sense that the account of it is based on a metaphorical dialectic of flight and entrapment: "The wings of her soul," we are told, "were broken," and "[e]xtreme unhappiness weighed visibly upon her" (421). But it is not so much as though Eustacia were burdened by some increase in the force of gravity as that she seems to be pulled downward by the deathly subterranean forces of the earth itself: she "sighed bitterly and ceased to stand erect, gradually crouching down under the umbrella as if she were drawn into the Barrow by a hand from beneath" (420). Then, as the downpour turns into a deluge, the operative metaphor becomes that of immersion, together with a steady waning of Eustacia's power of buoyancy:

> Between the drippings of the rain from her umbrella to her mantle, from her mantle to the heather, from the heather to the earth, very similar sounds could be heard coming from her lips; and the tearfulness of the outer scene was repeated upon her face . . . even had she seen herself . . . getting to Budmouth . . . she would have been but little more buoyant, so fearfully malignant were other things. (421)

Meanwhile, at Susan Nunsuch's cottage, fire seems to be no less malignant than water. The black magic directed against Eustacia there—Susan's making and burning of the beeswax doll—has the effect of completing the transformation of the natural forces of life into those of destruction, so that the whole elemental world appears intent on both drowning Eustacia and consuming her.

When, after a long silence, she finally resorts to speech, this resort is perceived as very much her last. "She uttered words aloud," the narrator announces with considerable portentousness: "When a woman in such a situation . . . takes upon herself to sob and soliloquize aloud there is something grievous the matter" (421). As "soliloquize" suggests, Eustacia's last words constitute part of a self-conscious tragic performance:

> "Can I go, can I go?" she moaned. "He's not great enough for me to give myself to—he does not suffice for my desire! . . . If he had been a Saul or a Bonaparte—ah! But to break my marriage vow for him—it is too poor a luxury! . . . And I have no money to go

alone! And if I could, what comfort to me? I must drag on next
year, as I have dragged on this year, and the year after that as
before." (421)

Words for Eustacia are almost totally theatrical, which means, among
other things, that they are chiefly rhetorical—just as Clym's words
were in the opening scenes of Book Fifth. But they do not give her, as
they gave Clym earlier, any relief from the pain of bondage, from her
perception of her life as simply a process of "dragging on" from one
year to the next.

Eustacia's words are rhetorical in that they amount to the striking of a pose, and yet this pose has real consequences. Her soliloquy
allows her in effect to see herself in such a way as to provide a clear
and compelling motivation for a course of action already instinctively
decided on:

> "How I have tried and tried to be a splendid woman, and how
> destiny has been against me! . . . I do not deserve my lot!" she
> cried in a frenzy of bitter revolt. "O, the cruelty of putting me
> into this ill-conceived world! I was capable of much; but I have
> been injured and blighted and crushed by things beyond my con-
> trol! O, how hard it is of Heaven to devise such tortures for me,
> who have done no harm to Heaven at all!" (421)

In a way, the question of the accuracy of this vision of herself and of
recent events seems to be beside the point. In light of such a vision,
what is most evident is that the only course of action left open to her
is the taking of her own life. Implicitly, Eustacia is demanding complete transcendence, and it can be argued that the sheer dramatic
impact of the last act she will perform gives her just that.

While Eustacia soliloquizes, Thomasin, who has been largely
absent from the narrative since her marriage to Wildeve, is also making an erratic journey across the heath. After having come to warn
Clym that her husband is preparing to run off with Eustacia, she, too,
is more than a little daunted by the sheer frenzy of the storm as she
decides to set off again for home: "To plunge into that medium was to
plunge into water slightly diluted with air" (429). Indeed, it is as if

Thomasin and her infant daughter, just as much as Eustacia, were in danger of being engulfed:

> Sometimes the path led her to hollows between thickets of tall and dripping bracken, dead, though not yet prostrate, which enclosed her like a pool. When they were more than usually tall she lifted the baby to the top of her head, that it might be out of the reach of their drenching fronds. On higher ground, where the wind was brisk and sustained, the rain flew in level flight without sensible descent, so that it was beyond all power to imagine the remoteness of the point at which it left the bosoms of the clouds. (429–30)

Thomasin's view of the deluge, however, is pointedly contrasted with Eustacia's:

> To her there were not, as to Eustacia, demons in the air, and malice in every bush and bough. The drops which lashed her face were not scorpions, but prosy rain; Egdon in the mass was no monster whatever, but impersonal open ground. Her fears of the place were rational, her dislikes of its worst moods reasonable. At this time it was in her view a windy, wet place, in which a person might experience much discomfort, lose the path without care, and possibly catch cold. (430)

The shift in perspective from the hysterical if exalted poetry of the soliloquy to Thomasin's "prosy" common sense is critical. Thomasin may be more stolid and less imaginative than Eustacia, but she is also less narcissistic and more sensitive to the pain of others. Action for her does not require the dimension of theatrical gesture to give it meaning. Like Diggory Venn, she is one of nature's survivors, one who quietly adapts to the conditions of her life rather than rebelling against them. She is the only one of the three women of Book First to survive the events of the narrative, and her daughter, embodying as she does the principle of life's continuity, represents the Yeobright family's hope for the future. Thomasin's relative lack of imagination and her capacity for compromise are in fact what sustain and ultimately save her. Without constantly demanding significance of the world, she accepts whatever constraints it imposes and operates within them as best she can.

At the same time, though, she lacks the heroic stature that Eustacia does manage, in the end, to achieve. Eustacia's very refusal to compromise with nature and circumstance gives her a tragic grandeur that allows her to transcend what had earlier been mere selfish egotism. Her drowning is almost certainly meant to be seen as an act of suicide, but even if we prefer to regard it as accidental, the strength of her desire for personal freedom and fulfillment takes her beyond the vanity of simple posturing. And yet this grandeur is finally inseparable from the idea of "performance," from her need even in defeat to play a significant part. In death itself, Eustacia is actually perceived in aesthetic terms, as if she were a great actress in the last scene of a classical tragedy. Besides Clym, her audience consists of Diggory and Charley,

> silently looking upon Eustacia, who, as she lay there . . . eclipsed all her living phases. Pallor did not include all the quality of her complexion, which seemed more than whiteness; it was almost light. The expression of her finely carved mouth was pleasant, as if a sense of dignity had just compelled her to leave off speaking. Eternal rigidity had seized upon it in a momentary transition between fervour and resignation. Her black hair was looser now than either of them had ever seen it before, and surrounded her brow like a forest. The stateliness of look which had been almost too marked for a dweller in a country domicile had at last found an artistically happy background. (442–43)

This last performance, in its statuesque immobility and silence—"as if a sense of dignity had just compelled her to leave off speaking"—suggests the kind of transcendent peace in which action has become as unnecessary as words.

It is not easy to decide whether Clym's fate is preferable to Eustacia's. "I am getting used to the horror of my existence" (444), he remarks bitterly at the end of Book Fifth. "[L]ooking like Lazarus coming from the tomb" (442), Clym has been resurrected from death. But, in effect disgorged, like Jonah, by the leviathan that has swallowed up

Eustacia, he finds himself deeply compromised by this re-emergence into the world of the living. "She is the second woman I have killed this year" (443), he cries, revealing a certain dramatic propensity of his own: "Those who ought to have lived lie dead; and here I am alive!" (443). In the circumstances, and even allowing for the kinds of virtue that Thomasin as a survivor embodies, there seems to be something almost morally suspect about the desire for survival itself. This something is hinted at in the fact that the arms of the drowned Wildeve were locked around Clym's legs when Diggory pulled the two of them out of the water, suggesting the innkeeper's last-minute desperation to save himself at all costs, and in the lacerations of his fingertips caused by his effort "to obtain a hold on the face of the weir-wall" (443).

This something, however, is dramatized most strikingly in the curious episode in which Diggory observes the nurse come downstairs, even while he still believes Clym to be dead, with "a rolled mass of wet paper" (441). This turns out to be the roll of banknotes with which Wildeve had planned to finance his flight with Eustacia. Stretching a couple of lengths of twine before the fire, and "unrolling the wet papers," the nurse "began pinning them one by one to the strings in a manner of clothes on a line" (441). Diggory watches "the steam from the double row of bank-notes as they waved backwards and forwards in the draught of the chimney till their flaccidity was changed to dry crispness throughout. Then the woman came and unpinned them, and, folding them together, carried the handful upstairs" (441–42).

The banknotes are obviously worth saving, but the nurse's attentiveness to them at this particular juncture has an odd and slightly repellent effect. Implicitly, their value seems to be placed nearly on a par with that of human life. Since the symbolic value of money is libidinal energy, epitomizing the pride of life itself, there is nothing too surprising about this; yet the note of prudent materialism in the nurse's action seems not quite in harmony with the general tenor of the occasion. His money is what survives of Damon Wildeve, but this survival underlines the fact that money is impersonal, its value absolutely independent of that of the man who owned it. Money survives as a thing in itself, so to speak, ultimately distinct from the aspirations of any one person. In other words, the life blood of human affairs goes on circulating with only tenuous and temporary links to particular human hearts. And when money is perceived as surviving in this way, the significance of human survival is somehow diminished. Here the money is not even dignified by its taking the form of jewels or even guineas: it consists merely of crisp but rather crassly prosaic banknotes.

The effect is, if not quite to debase the value of survival itself, then certainly to heighten our sense of the unique and vital worth of the one person who no longer had any wish to survive. Even if it was accidental, Eustacia's plunge into Shadwater Weir changes her status from that of social outsider to that of sacrificial victim. Eustacia seems ennobled in death precisely because she has died with such contempt for the state of bondage she had learned to envision as intrinsic to life. Under the terms of this vision she has offered herself up to the "colossal animal," and such an offering is perceived, inevitably, as an act of tragic propitiation. Clym's bitter intimation that it is she who has paid the price for his survival becomes an obsession in Book Sixth, and the celebration of the general renewal of eros and life in "Aftercourses" has the effect of seeming to be something more than a merely indirect result of the final part Eustacia has played.

9

"Aftercourses": A Catastrophic Dash

But everywhere he was kindly received, for the story of his life had
become generally known.

Quite apart from considerations of artistic structure, the exigencies
of Victorian serial publication made it virtually impossible for Hardy
to have ended his novel with the tragic death of Eustacia Vye: all the
pressures of the contemporary marketplace in fiction were for a less
morbid and more hopeful kind of ending. Regardless of such external demands, however, purely structural considerations did in fact
suggest the need for some sort of epilogue. For one thing, a number
of loose ends pertaining to both character and plot—like the future
of Thomasin and, indeed, of Diggory Venn—are left dangling at the
conclusion of Book Fifth. More to the point in artistic terms, though,
the finality represented by Eustacia's death works against the grain of
a crucial structural element in the novel—that of the peculiarly influential effect of the movement of time in relation to life on Egdon
Heath. In most kinds of realistic fiction time functions more or less
sequentially, as if it were a straight horizontal line that might safely be
assumed to continue after the story is over. In *The Return of the*

Native, however, time constitutes an unusually significant dimension, not so much in its forward linear thrust as in the circular impetus of its seasonal, and sometimes even its daily, cycles. The temporal rhythms in this story are conspicuously cyclical, and the inexorably ongoing nature of these repeated rhythms needs somehow to be accommodated by any principle of closure.

There is much talk in Book Sixth of time in relation to stories. Clym, for example, finds a sort of melancholy comfort, not only in his view of the heath as a text but in the "tale" that this text tells about the rise and fall of human cultures and their aspirations of permanence:

> He frequently walked the heath alone, when the past seized upon him with its shadowy hand, and held him there to listen to its tale. His imagination would then people the spot with its ancient inhabitants: forgotten Celtic tribes trod their tracks about him, and he could almost live among them, look in their faces, and see them standing beside the barrows which swelled around, untouched and perfect as at the time of their erection. Those of the dyed barbarians who had chosen the cultivable tracts were, in comparison with those who had left their marks here, as writers on paper beside writers on parchment. Their records had perished long ago by the plough, while the works of these remained. Yet they all had lived and died unconscious of the different fates awaiting their relics. It reminded him that unforeseen factors operate in the evolution of immortality. (449)

Burial mounds, even viewed in the light of "marks" left on "parchment," are of course rather odd manifestations of immortality; but one of the most striking revelations of Book Sixth is that this type of fiction-making—by no means unique to Clym—always tends to deal in just that type of permanence.

"The story of the deaths of Eustacia and Wildeve," we learn in the opening sentence of "Aftercourses," "was told throughout Egdon, and far beyond, for many weeks and months":

> All the known incidents of their love were enlarged, distorted, touched up, and modified, till the original reality bore but a slight

resemblance to the counterfeit presentation by surrounding tongues. Yet, upon the whole, neither the man nor the woman lost dignity by sudden death. Misfortune had struck them gracefully, cutting off their erratic histories with a catastrophic dash, instead of, as with many, attenuating each life to an uninteresting meagreness, through long years of wrinkles, neglect, and decay. (447)

The "catastrophic dash" that bestows a distinctive significance and thus a kind of permanence on the lives of Eustacia and Wildeve also suggests that such stories, while not entirely falsifying reality, have a way of making it seem paradoxically static. Among other things, the fictionalizing of reality is a process of restructuring the normal rhythms of time, often in such a way as to isolate a significant moment by arresting or seeming to "freeze" it in the sequential flow—a procedure that depends largely, however, on the perception of time as a process of cyclical repetition.

The most famous instance of this is perhaps the vision of the kind of transcendent immortality implicit in the story depicted on Keats's Grecian urn. Such a vision can take more sinister forms, too, of course, as in, for example, the gruesome isolation and perpetuation of a highly significant moment in William Faulkner's short story "A Rose for Emily." At any rate, to the extent that Clym Yeobright can be consoled for his losses, it is precisely his sense of the ancient burial mounds as somehow frozen in time that consoles him. He tries to imagine all the lost cycles of history that lie behind or beneath the barrows; but if the movement of time is cyclical, then, by the very nature of the inevitable recurrence of its rhythms, it also involves an important element of stasis, so that nothing in even the most "erratic" of "histories" can ever be entirely lost. The element of temporal stasis, paradoxically, is always implicit in the narrative flow of storymaking.

There is also much talk in Book Sixth, however, of time in relation not to stories but to the experience of ordinary reality. The first chapter is entitled "The Inevitable Movement Onward," and despite an initial preoccupation with the discontinuous fictive "dash" that has ended the histories of Eustacia and Wildeve, Book Sixth seems to be primarily concerned with the linear ongoingness of life itself. Whereas Clym is linked to the stasis of "story," Thomasin is associated with the more familiar perception of time as the sequential continuity of past, present, and future. "[T]he horrors of the unknown had passed" (447) for Thomasin, we are told: "The spring came and calmed her; the summer came and soothed her; the autumn arrived, and she began to be comforted, for her little girl was strong and happy, growing in size and knowledge every day" (448). Although she goes to live with Clym at Blooms-End, the legacy of Wildeve's money gives her a new measure of independence and freedom. Time heals as well as destroys, and when the next winter arrives she has "laid her heart open to external influences of every kind" (449). The implied contrast here is between the vision of Eustacia's final mute immobility and Thomasin's lively capacity for movement and change. While there may be something inartistic and even morally compromising about the inevitability of the movement onward, people must adapt to it if they are to continue to live.

Clym's existence, on the other hand, as indicated by his obsession with both the remote and the recent past, becomes an attempt to avoid the ongoingness of time. Glad though he is to have Thomasin living with him, he is in a sense isolated and immured in a self-imposed stasis. "Confining" himself "to two rooms at the top of the back staircase, where he lived on quietly . . . going his own ways, and thinking his own thoughts" (448), he becomes aware of Thomasin's renewed life "only in the form of sounds through a wood partition as he sat over books of exceptionally large type" (449). Besides his haunting of the barrows, Clym's only other activity until now has been to visit the graves of his mother and Eustacia. Given his new domestic arrangements, though, the possibility that he himself could become the most important of the external influences to which his cousin has laid open her heart is fairly clear, and the great unspoken question at first seems to be whether he will at last have enough sense to ask her to marry him. But Clym's withdrawal, his lack of interest either in the present or in any promise that the future might be thought to hold, makes the question academic even before the reappearance, with the coming of the following summer, of Diggory Venn.

The account of Diggory's return to Egdon recapitulates the inside/outside motif that we have seen before in the novel. One summer day, as Clym is "in the garden, immediately outside the parlour-window, which was as usual open" (450), he hears "a slight scream from Thomasin, who was sitting inside the room" (450). "O, how you frightened me!" she cries; "I thought you were the ghost of yourself" (450). The scene is constructed in such a way that it is Clym who appears initially to be this "ghost": it is as if he has become not merely an outsider now but virtually a phantom in his own world. "To his astonishment," however, when he looks "in at the window,"

> there stood within the room Diggory Venn, no longer a reddleman, but exhibiting the strangely altered hues of an ordinary Christian countenance, white shirt-front, light flowered waistcoat, blue-spotted neckerchief, and bottle-green coat. Nothing in this appearance was at all singular but the fact of its great difference from what he had formerly been. Red, and all approach to red, was carefully excluded from every article of clothes upon him. (450)

The most dramatic aspect of Diggory's transformation into a prosperous dairy farmer is the disappearance of the red dye that had stained him from head to toe. Clym's amazement, when he joins the other two in the parlor, is exceeded only by Thomasin's: "I was so alarmed!" she explains, "smiling from one to the other. 'I couldn't believe that he had got white of his own accord! It seemed supernatural'" (450). She continues to make much of this development: "How did you manage to become so white, Diggory?" she asks; when she goes on to tell him, "You look much better than ever you did before" (451), Diggory's confusion and her own blushes make it clear that there has suddenly been a transformation of their old friendship as well. Though Clym, we are told, "saw nothing of this" (451), the new Diggory has evidently come courting, and his attentions are not at all unwelcome.

With his ghostly pallor, it is as if Diggory has in fact returned from the world of the dead. His return has been viewed as problematic by some critics, a view perhaps prompted but at any rate apparently supported by Hardy's curious extranarrative footnote on the subject at the end of Chapter 3 in the 1912 Wessex edition:

> The writer may state here that the original conception of the story did not designate a marriage between Thomasin and Venn. He was to have retained his isolated and weird character to the last, and to have disappeared mysteriously from the heath, nobody knowing whither—Thomasin remaining a widow. But certain circumstances of serial publication led to a change of intent. (464)

The statement seems quite unambiguous, indicating not only Hardy's preference for an "original conception" of Diggory as a much more enigmatic character than he appears to be in Book Sixth, but also a kind of ultimate theoretical preference for tragedy. But it is difficult to know what "the original conception of the story" means in this context: the earliest drafts of the novel, in which Eustacia figures as an actual witch, are so different from the final form of the story as to make it almost impossible to imagine how the original notion of Diggory could be accommodated to the plot as it eventually developed and presently stands.[16]

In structural terms, at any rate, Book Sixth as we now have it makes at least as much sense as any putative ending—a much abbreviated "Aftercourses," presumably. It is also difficult to imagine any significant plot development beyond the climax in Book Fifth—in which Diggory simply vanishes, and Thomasin remains a widow. "Readers," Hardy's footnote continues, "can therefore choose between the endings, and those with an austere artistic code can assume the more consistent conclusion to be the true one" (464). But consistent with what? It seems unlikely that a rather vaguely sketched-out conclusion that might have been consistent with the original version of the plot would in fact be consistent with the vastly different final version.

Even if, by "the original conception of the story," Hardy is referring to the final form of the plot, the implicitly dim view that he takes of his own published ending is not terribly persuasive. Robert Heilman argues that "[t]here is no artistic softening-up in the story of [Diggory's] and Thomasin's marrying," that "Hardy is simply wrong" about this (Heilman, 79). Michael Millgate expresses similar doubts about the footnote, pointing out that the published ending "has a 'rightness' of its own."[17] This rightness has to do, of course, with the fact that it works against the principle of the "catastrophic dash," against the kind of stasis represented by the burial mounds. And the ending as we have it manages to assimilate the idea of the ongoing-ness of time, not just in its linear progression but also in its cyclical aspect. The mythic dimension in the novel's structure dictates the need for a period of rebirth and renewal consequent on the deaths of Eustacia and Wildeve, a summer phase following winter's desolation and sterility.

Hardy's real problem with Book Sixth seems to be that whereas he had set out to write a tragedy, he found himself, by the end, writing a kind of romance. But his genuine gift as a novelist was not so much for tragedy as for irony, and at the end of *The Return of the Native* it is only through the genre of pastoral romance, paradoxically, that irony becomes available to him. To put it another way, the more "aus-tere" ending is the one that Clym Yeobright, given the chance, so to speak, might himself have chosen, and it is even in a sense the one that he tries somehow to realize in what remains of his own life.

Diggory and Thomasin are clearly well matched, but Clym sees "nothing of this" precisely because he so seldom sees any reality set clearly before his eyes. At the realistic level of plot, the deaths of Eustacia and Wildeve have the positive effect of allowing Diggory and Thomasin to come together; at the mythic level, Eustacia's death in particular has what might be termed a redemptive function. In losing his redness, the mark of the wandering outcast, Diggory rejoins the life of the human community, not so much on Egdon as in the more fertile regions adjoining it. But even on Egdon, a green world, echoing that of Book Third, has also been restored. In the context of the legend of Saint George and the dragon, the hero has failed to rescue the threat-ened maiden, but it is as if the sacrifice of Eustacia has appeased the "colossal animal" for the time being and permitted all the other char-acters to be restored to new life. The sole exception here is in a sense the hero himself, for Clym has no interest in being so restored—the ongoing movement of his own life has ended with Eustacia's death. The final, terrible irony of the novel is that it is as if in fact Clym does not realize what has happened, does not understand that his sterile bondage to the past and to the world of death is self-willed. He emerges from the jaws of the dragon to preach "the eleventh commandment" of love, but as far as his own static existence is concerned, love seems to be the farthest thing from his mind.

In view of the fact that the general renewal of life on the heath is perceived in terms that are specifically erotic and romantic, the irony in Clym's idea that he needs to become a preacher of the eleventh commandment is dramatized in a particularly vivid way. The phallic Maypole, for example, is the central emblem of the dominant motif of pastoral romance in Book Sixth. The morning after Diggory's visit,

> when Thomasin withdrew the curtains of her bedroom window, there stood the Maypole in the middle of the green, its top cutting into the sky. It had sprung up in the night . . . like Jack's beanstalk. She opened the casement to get a better view of the garlands and posies that adorned it. The sweet perfume of the flowers had already spread into the surrounding air, which, being free from every taint, conducted to her lips a full measure of the fragrance received from the spire of blossom in its midst. At the top of the pole were crossed hoops decked with small flowers; beneath these came a milk-white zone of Maybloom; then a zone of bluebells, then of cowslips, then of lilacs, then of ragged-robins, daffodils, and so on, till the lowest stage was reached. Thomasin noticed all these, and was delighted that the May-revel was to be so near. (452)

The celebration of the return of summer, with all its sexual undertones, is exemplified as well in the sudden blossoming of Thomasin herself: "She was dressed more gaily than Yeobright had ever seen her dress since the time of Wildeve's death, eighteen months before; since the day of her marriage even she had not exhibited herself to such advantage" (452). Startled, Clym misreads the situation, wondering first if it might be "possible that she had put on her summer clothes to please him" and then feeling "almost . . . troubled at the thought of it" (453). For

> [e]very pulse of loverlike feeling which had not been stilled during Eustacia's lifetime had gone into the grave with her. His passion for her had occurred too far on in his manhood to leave fuel

enough on hand for another fire of that sort, as may happen with
more boyish loves. Even supposing him capable of loving again,
that love would be a plant of slow and laboured growth, and in
the end only small and sickly, like an autumn-hatched bird. (453)

The contrast between this stunted "plant" and the profusion of brilliant foliage decorating the Maypole makes it painfully clear to the
reader that Thomasin's own transformation has been inspired by
another source altogether. Nevertheless, distressed as much by what is
now his conviction that she has adorned herself for his benefit as by
the arrival of the brass band signaling the start of the May festivities,
Clym makes a panicky retreat: "he withdrew from his rooms by the
back door, went down the garden, through the gate in the hedge, and
away out of sight. He could not bear to remain in the presence of
enjoyment to-day, though he had tried hard" (453).

Clym is always vanishing in this way in Book Sixth, so much so,
in fact, that he remains totally oblivious of the courting rituals of
Diggory and Thomasin. These rituals are as elaborately opaque as
those in any mating dance, yet at the same time they have a remarkably forthright and even businesslike air as well. There is always a play-
fully circuitous quality about the flirtatiousness of the couple, as in, for
instance, their behavior during Diggory's moonlight search "for a
glove that was dropped by one of the maidens" (454) at the Maypole
dance: "To think," Thomasin exclaims, before she has learned that the
glove is her own, "that a man should be so silly as to go mooning
about like that. . . . A respectable dairyman, too, and a man of money
as he is now. What a pity!" (455). But this kind of romantic deviousness is in fact underlaid by a much more direct and straightforward
quality in each of them. After Diggory's zigzagging search for the
glove, he kisses it when he has found it, puts it in his breast-pocket,
then quickly makes his way "in a mathematically direct line towards
his distant home in the meadows" (455). He does not wander or "lose
the path": Diggory knows exactly where he is going. When he reap-
pears on horseback some days later, as Thomasin is playing with her
little girl on the heath, her own behavior is equally characteristic:
"'Diggory, give me my glove,' said Thomasin, whose manner it was

under any circumstances to plunge into the midst of a subject which engrossed her" (457).

A discussion about his "feelings" (458) ensues, in which, despite some mutual reversions into indirection and playfulness, Diggory is concerned to let her know that he is a man of substantial means now, his eligibility as a prospective husband in no doubt. Thomasin also tells him about the exact disposition of her own inherited wealth, and although he feigns a lack of romantic ardor, the scene features a practical exchange of hard information as well as flirtatious dalliance: "I don't know much what feelings are now-a-days," Diggory claims, disingenuously; "I have got so mixed up with business of one sort and t'other that my soft sentiments are gone off in vapour like. Yes, I am given up body and soul to the making of money. Money is all my dream" (458). The conversation occurs, significantly, near the almost "mathematically direct line" of the old Roman road, and this becomes their tacitly agreed meeting place from now on. The contrast between the way they conduct themselves and the brand of romantic deviousness formerly exhibited by Eustacia Vye is much more marked than any similarity: our sense of the novel's world as dangerously labyrinthine has now vanished as completely as Clym Yeobright has (for the time being at least) from the narrative.

The mating dance of Thomasin and Diggory has a sort of pragmatic innocence that was missing from the more calculated performances of Eustacia, the story having moved into the benign world of pure pastoral idyll. As the episode in which the rustics make a marriage bed for the couple on their wedding day suggests, this phase is both erotic and comic. The scene involves much of the same type of sexual innuendo, particularly on the part of the indefatigable Grandfer Cantle, that had characterized the local response to the "failed" wedding in Book First, but it is much more lighthearted, and entirely free of the earlier sense of ominousness. And what had been a portent of death in Book Fifth becomes an image of fertility here: just as the same kind of patch of shepherd's thyme on which Mrs. Yeobright had collapsed becomes a place of romantic rendezvous for Diggory and Thomasin, so a lump of beeswax—something that had been linked to Eustacia's destruction—is now associated with the energy of sexual renewal.

The idyll differs from that in Book Fourth, however, the one following the wedding of Clym and Eustacia, in that it is marked by the distinctively festive mood of pastoral comedy. As Timothy Fairway waxes the "bed-tick" the vast paper bags full of goosefeathers for stuffing it soon turn the room into a place both of comic confusion and of near magical wonder: "airy tufts of down and feathers floated about the room in increasing quantity till, through a mishap of Christian's, who shook the contents of one bag outside the tick, the atmosphere . . . became dense with gigantic flakes, which descended upon the workers like a windless snowstorm" (466). At this point Hardy even reveals a perhaps unexpected talent for the note of benign whimsy that so often typifies this kind of pastoral: "They sat down to lunch in the midst of their work, feathers around, above, and below them; the original owners of which occasionally came to the open door and cackled begrudgingly at sight of such a quantity of old clothes" (468).

The one character who does not participate in all this revelry is Clym. Long after the central romantic situation in Book Sixth has become clear to everyone else, Clym is still dithering solemnly about his obligations to his mother's memory—specifically, about whether Mrs. Yeobright's former hopes with respect to himself and Thomasin now make it his "duty" to remarry:

> Throughout this period Yeobright had more or less pondered on his duty to his cousin Thomasin. He could not help feeling that it would be a pitiful waste of sweet material if the tender-natured thing should be doomed from this early stage of her life onwards to dribble away her winsome qualities on lonely gorse and fern. But he felt this as an economist merely, and not as a lover. His passion for Eustacia had been a sort of conserve of his whole life, and he had nothing more of that supreme quality left to bestow. So far the obvious thing was not to entertain any idea of marriage with Thomasin, even to oblige her. (460)

Clym believes that he must honor "a dead mother's hope" (460), but dreads contemplating "Thomasin wedded to the mere corpse of a lover that he now felt himself to be" (460). Nevertheless, he finally decides to propose:

> It was even with a pleasant sense of doing his duty that he went downstairs to her one evening for this purpose, when the sun was printing on the valley the same long shadow of the housetop that he had seen lying there times out of number while his mother lived. (461)

This image of the sun "printing" the shadow of the house suggests Clym's habit not only of textualizing his world but also of reading it in an odd way. It underlines the intensity of his commitment to the stasis represented by the past: to the extent that the "text" had been inscribed like this "times out of number," then Mrs. Yeobright's life and maternal authority can be seen as having acquired the same kind of permanence conferred on the shadow by the principle of cyclical repetition in time. From Clym's point of view, in other words, his obligation to his mother's memory remains unmodified by anything so insubstantial as a sense of life's ongoingness; what the shadow signifies is for him more important than any living and changing reality in the house itself.

He is more relieved than dismayed, however, when Thomasin, anticipating his intention, forestalls him in his duty by asking to be allowed to "speak first" (461), and tells him that she wants to marry someone else. In this, she exhibits her usual combination of forthrightness and tact. Clym is less pleased when he learns that the object of her affections is Diggory, and his response might be regarded as perpetuating as well as echoing the unattractive streak of snobbishness that had also been one of the immutable features of his mother's character. But his sense of relief eventually wins out even over this, with some assistance from a display of stubbornness by Thomasin, which, though it surprises him, seems to come from the same familial source. And by the time the wedding day arrives, it is no longer so much that Clym has been reconciled to the idea of the marriage as that he has merely lost interest in it. Again, he simply withdraws from the festivities, going first to his room to write a sermon and then for a walk on the heath, where he meets Charley.

The friendship that springs up between these two presents us with a curious paradox just prior to the novel's conclusion: it reveals that Clym is at once much younger and much older than his years. The basis of the affinity is their shared romantic melancholy, which derives from a mutual obsession with Eustacia; but while this seems not entirely inappropriate in a lovestricken adolescent like Charley, in Clym it suggests something more like hysterical fixation. Clym has always evinced a certain childish inflexibility of character; now he seems to exemplify nothing less than arrested development. Charley's obsession becomes an image of Clym's, and it presents the older man's behavior on his cousin's wedding day in a strange and pathetic light. Conscious of themselves as outsiders when they return to a darkened Blooms-End—for "the shutters were closed, so that nothing of the interior could be seen" (471)—they go up to Clym's sitting-room, where he presents Charley with one of Eustacia's "undulating locks of raven hair" (471).

The boy's sobbing gratitude for this memento, understandable enough in itself, suddenly dramatizes not just the pathos but the immaturity of Clym's singlemindedness: Charley "kissed the packet, put it in his pocket, and said in a voice of emotion, 'O, Mr. Clym, how good you are to me!'" (471). It is as if Clym has become not so much the preacher of the eleventh commandment of love as a kind of priest in a youthful romantic cult of death. At the same time, it is as if he is not so much a very young man himself as a very old one. After they have left the house there is a final recapitulation of the inside/outside motif when they pause at a window to peer in at the wedding party: "what are they doing?" Clym asks Charley; "My sight is weaker again tonight, and the glass of this window is not good" (471). The effect, with Charley describing the interior celebrations as to a blind man, is to suggest the frailty and the isolation of old age.

For Clym's life does indeed seem to be virtually over. He spends the rest of the evening in the dark and now deserted house, communing—almost a ghost himself—with the ghostly memories of Mrs. Yeobright and Eustacia. But his isolation, if not his frailty, is self-imposed. His fixation has to do with death rather than with love, with the stasis of the "catastrophic dash"—a textual sign that refuses to yield any humanly intelligible meaning. When we next see him, he appears at first to be alone again, "a motionless figure standing on top of [Rainbarrow], just as Eustacia had stood on that lonely summit some two years and a half before" (473). He is not alone, as it turns out, but he might as well be: delivering "the first of a series of moral lectures or Sermons on the Mount," he addresses a sparse Sunday afternoon gathering that, while listening to his words, "abstractedly pulled heather, stripped ferns, or tossed pebbles down the slope" (473).

Unlike the original Sermon on the Mount, this one does not strike any responsive sparks from its audience; in his isolation Clym seems rather to be a source of pity than of fervor or inspiration. Even the biblical text on which his sermon is based—an episode from the Book of Kings apparently chosen to exemplify the importance of filial love, in this case, that of Solomon for his mother, Bathsheba—involves an ironic subtext that has to do not with love but with death: in the biblical story Solomon not only does not grant Bathsheba's request to allow his elder brother to marry but in fact has him killed instead. Once again, Clym's moral gloss on one of the key events in his own life is based on what could be described as a confused reading.

Ironically, too, Clym ends up by becoming in a way what Eustacia had always been—a kind of performer. He speaks

> not only in simple language on Rainbarrow and in the hamlets round, but in a more cultivated strain elsewhere—from the steps and porticoes of town-halls, from market-crosses, from conduits, on esplanades and on wharves, from the parapets of bridges, in barns and outhouses, and all other such places in the neighbouring Wessex towns and villages. He left alone creeds and systems of philosophy, finding enough and more than enough to occupy his tongue in the opinions and actions common to all good men. Some believed him, and some believed not; some said that his words were commonplace, others complained of his want of theological doctrine; while others again remarked that it was well enough for a man to take to preaching who could not see to do anything else. But everywhere he was kindly received, for the story of his life had become generally known. (474)

While his performances receive what might be charitably regarded as only mixed reviews, it is the "story" underlying them that keeps the audiences coming back. According to his preaching scheme, "his texts would be taken from all kinds of books" (474), but in the last analysis the only "text" that matters is the one that he has made of his own life. The trouble, however, with a phrase like "the story of his life" is that it implies completion or closure: the sad fact by the end of the novel is that in effect Clym's life is already ended as well.

Not only does Clym decline to participate in the renewal of the forces of eros and fertility in Book Sixth, he hardly appears even to notice them. For himself, he has chosen the stasis of "story"; life of course goes on without him, but he does not quite notice that either. And this ultimate failure of recognition is very much in alignment with all the other ironies in the novel. Hardy's aspiration was always to write a fictional equivalent of classical tragedy, but tragedy in his work, like romance at the end of *The Return of the Native,* is always, finally, in the service of irony. In this, perhaps, more than in anything else, Hardy can be regarded as no less a modern than a Victorian novelist.

By its very nature, irony is essentially parody-romance, and in this respect the structural organizing principle in *The Return of the Native* is not very different from that in a classic modernist text like James Joyce's *Ulysses.* Clym Yeobright's character is conceived as much in terms of the principle of ironic parody as that of Leopold Bloom. In his final Sermon on the Mount scene he is perceived quite explicitly as a parodic Christ figure; more fundamentally, however, he is an impotent Saint George, an obtuse and ineffectual version of Spenser's Redcross Knight. It is not, though, that Hardy is merely deriding Clym; he is offering him in fact as a type of modern everyman, an intellectual idealist who has lost touch with the living vitality of his own culture—not so much through any inherent personal deficiency as through a combination of historical and evolutionary forces beyond his control. The development of the kind of high rationality that Clym represents virtually dooms him, paradoxically perhaps, as an antagonist of the "colossal animal" represented by Egdon Heath. Whether we choose to regard the operative principle of malevolence in the novel as a cosmic "immanent will"—to use the phrase that

Hardy later borrowed from Schopenhauer—or merely as the power of nature and chance over human desire, Clym is not the hero who could ever have overcome it.

If anyone does come close to being a dragon slayer it is Diggory Venn—or, more accurately, Diggory in combination, so to speak, with Thomasin. In the Spenserian analogy the "whitened" Diggory is like the Redcross Knight finally restored to the fullness of life: he "rescues" Thomasin in the end, but Thomasin can be seen as a Una figure who, by virtue of her love, also rescues him. As characters, Diggory and Thomasin, even if they are more limited and less interesting than Clym and Eustacia, are more rooted in and better adapted to their world. For all that Clym tries to make a virtue of returning to his native home, he no longer quite belongs there. He remains as deracinated as he had felt himself to be in Paris, becoming in his own way almost as much one of nature's exiles as Eustacia. And this essential rootlessness saps his energies. If Eustacia's tragedy has to do with an excess of Promethean longing, the irony implicit in Clym's much heralded return derives from a steady dwindling, not of noble intentions, but of sheer vitality. The native of Egdon Heath ends up virtually as dead as the woman whose life had been devoted to escaping it.

Notes and References

1. *The Return of the Native*, ed. George Woodcock (Harmondsworth, England: Penguin English Library, 1978), 233; page numbers cited hereafter in text.

2. See J. Garver, *Thomas Hardy: The Return of the Native* (London: Penguin, 1988), 60–61. Much of what follows in this chapter is elaborated in greater detail by Garver, 50–74.

3. The organization of this chapter owes much to Charles Lock's *Criticism in Focus: Thomas Hardy* (New York: St. Martin's Press, 1992).

4. Rosemarie Morgan, *Women and Sexuality in the Novels of Thomas Hardy* (London: Routledge, 1988), 75.

5. See, for example, Richard Carpenter, *Thomas Hardy* (New York: Twayne Publishers, 1964), 97–98; Jean R. Brooks, "*The Return of the Native*: A Novel of Environment," in *Thomas Hardy's "The Return of the Native,"* Modern Critical Interpretations, ed. Harold Bloom (New York: Chelsea House, 1987), 29–30; and Peter J. Casagrande, "Son and Lover: The Dilemma of Clym Yeobright" in *Thomas Hardy: The Tragic Novels*, A Casebook, ed. R. P. Draper (London: Macmillan Education, 1991), 117.

6. Northrop Frye, *The Great Code: The Bible and Literature* (Orlando, Fla.: Harvest/HBJ, 1983), 187–88.

7. Irving Howe, "*The Return of the Native*" in *Thomas Hardy's The Return of the Native*, Modern Critical Interpretations, ed. Harold Bloom (New York: Chelsea House, 1987), 18.

8. Robert B. Heilman, "*The Return*: Centennial Observations" in *The Novels of Thomas Hardy*, ed. Anne Smith (London: Vision Press, 1979), 72.

9. T. R. Wright, *Hardy and the Erotic* (London: Macmillan, 1989), 59.

10. J. B. Bullen, *The Expressive Eye: Fiction and Perception in the Work of Thomas Hardy* (Oxford: Clarendon Press, 1986), 109.

11. Marlene Springer, *Hardy's Use of Allusion* (London: Macmillan, 1983), 117.

12. For a more extensive account of Hardy's "bifocal" method of characterization, see Ian Gregor, *The Great Web: The Form of Hardy's Major Fiction* (London: Faber & Faber, 1974).

13. J. Hillis Miller, *Thomas Hardy: Distance and Desire* (Cambridge, Mass.: Harvard University Press, 1970), 169.

14. Joseph Warren Beach, *The Technique of Thomas Hardy* (Chicago: University of Chicago Press, 1922).

15. Rosemary Sumner, *Thomas Hardy: Psychological Novelist* (London: Macmillan, 1981), 106.

16. For a full account of the original composition of the novel and Hardy's processes of revision, see John Paterson, *The Making of "The Return of the Native"* (Berkeley: University of California Press, 1960).

17. Michael Millgate, *Thomas Hardy: His Career as a Novelist* (London: Bodley Head, 1971), 142.

Selected Bibliography

Primary Works

The Return of the Native. Edited with an introduction and notes by George Woodcock. Harmondsworth, England: Penguin English Library, 1978. Reprint of Macmillan Wessex Edition of 1912.

Secondary Works

Beach, Joseph Warren. *The Technique of Thomas Hardy.* Chicago: University of Chicago Press, 1922. The first important study of Hardy's narrative technique; considers the dramatic structure of *The Return.*

Berger, Sheila. *Thomas Hardy and Visual Structures: Framing, Disruption, Process.* New York: New York University Press, 1990. Studies Hardy's visual techniques and argues that meanings are not fixed or static in the novels; sees the ending of *The Return* as deliberately intrusive and implausible, so as to expose the nineteenth-century idea of closure as inadequate.

Brooks, Jean R. "*The Return of the Native*: A Novel of Environment." In *Thomas Hardy's "The Return of the Native,"* Modern Critical Interpretations, edited by Harold Bloom. New York: Chelsea House, 1987. Considers the novel's mythic structure.

Bullen, J. B. *The Expressive Eye: Fiction and Perception in the Work of Thomas Hardy.* Oxford: Clarendon Press, 1986. Considers Hardy's visual techniques, especially in relation to his knowledge of painting and art history.

Carpenter, Richard. *Thomas Hardy*. New York: Twayne Publishers, 1964. Discusses the centrality of myth in Hardy's fiction; sees Clym Yeobright as a modern ironic version of an archetypal mythic hero.

Casagrande, Peter J. "Son and Lover: The Dilemma of Clym Yeobright." In *Thomas Hardy: The Tragic Novels*, A Casebook, edited by R. P. Draper. London: Macmillan Education, 1991. Sees Clym's attempt to secure redemption through return as a failure and demonstrates that Johnny Nunsuch and Christian Cantle are Clym's narrative counterparts.

Firor, Ruth. *Folkways in Thomas Hardy*. Philadelphia: University of Pennsylvania Press, 1931. An important study of Hardy's use of local myth and legend; particularly informative on the mummers' Saint George play in *The Return*.

Garson, Marjorie. *Hardy's Fables of Integrity: Woman, Body, Text*. Oxford: Clarendon Press, 1991. An insightful feminist and Lacanian reading of seven Hardy novels; sees Clym's self-perception as fragmented and stresses his dependency on Mrs. Yeobright.

Garver, J. *Thomas Hardy: The Return of the Native*. London: Penguin Books, 1988. A close reading of the novel that includes much useful information about its historical and cultural context.

Gregor, Ian. *The Great Web: The Form of Hardy's Major Fiction*. London: Faber & Faber, 1974. Considers the form of the major novels in terms of the idea of "process"; discusses apparent incongruities of characterization in *The Return* in relation to Hardy's "bifocal" technique.

Guerard, Albert J. *Thomas Hardy*. New York: New Directions, 1964. Considers Hardy as a "modern" novelist and discusses the ways in which his novels depart from nineteenth-century conventions of realism.

Heilman, Robert B. "*The Return*: Centennial Observations." In *The Novels of Thomas Hardy*, edited by Anne Smith. London: Vision Press, 1979. An illuminating essay on the novel; takes issue with the idea in Hardy's footnote in the Wessex Edition that the novel's ending represents an artistic compromise.

Holloway, John. "Hardy's Major Fiction." In *Hardy: A Collection of Critical Essays*, edited by Albert J. Guerard. Englewood Cliffs, N.J.: Prentice-Hall, 1963. Examines the tension between the older rural way of life and the effects of modernity in *The Return* and other novels.

Howe, Irving. "*The Return of the Native*." In *Thomas Hardy's "The Return of the Native,"* Modern Critical Interpretations, edited by Harold Bloom. New York: Chelsea House, 1987. A perceptive reading of the novel that suggests the idea of Clym's sexual impotence.

Kramer, Dale. *Thomas Hardy: The Forms of Tragedy*. Detroit: Wayne State University Press, 1975. Examines the tragic structure of *The Return* in the context of the relation between perception and meaning.

Lawrence, D. H. "Study of Thomas Hardy." In *Phoenix*. London: Heinemann, 1936. Discusses the centrality of Egdon Heath in *The Return;* sees it as a symbol of dark natural instinct, a force that is repressed in Clym and embodied by Eustacia.

Miller, J. Hillis. *Thomas Hardy: Distance and Desire*. Cambridge, Mass.: Harvard University Press, 1970. An important study that discusses the tension between distance and desire in Hardy's novels; sees the country dance in *The Return* as a definitive emblem of this tension. A seminal work for feminist and deconstructionist readings of the novel.

Millgate, Michael. *Thomas Hardy: His Career as a Novelist*. London: Bodley Head, 1971. A comprehensive study that emphasizes Hardy's professionalism. Sees *The Return* as lacking in technical sophistication; regards Clym as a highly unsympathetic character. Like Heilman, expresses doubts about Hardy's footnote in Book Sixth.

Mitchell, Judith. "Hardy's Female Reader." In *The Sense of Sex: Feminist Perspectives on Hardy,* edited by Margaret R. Higonnet. Urbana and Chicago: University of Illinois Press, 1993. Examines the visualizations of the female protagonists in the novels and argues that the objectifications of Eustacia make it impossible for the narrator to depict her as an erotic subject.

Morrell, Roy. *Thomas Hardy: The Will and the Way*. Kuala Lumpur: University of Malaya Press, 1965. Examines Hardy's philosophical ideas and shows how these are modified in the process of imaginative assimilation in the novels.

Paterson, John. *The Making of "The Return of the Native."* Berkeley: University of California Press, 1960. Traces the textual history of the manuscript, showing how drastically the final version differs from Hardy's original conception.

Springer, Marlene. *Hardy's Use of Allusion*. London: Macmillan, 1983. Shows how Hardy's allusiveness in *The Return* is integral to the novel's structure. Sees Clym as a victim of the fantasies of his idealism and as unable to comprehend Eustacia's passions and needs.

Sumner, Rosemary. *Thomas Hardy: Psychological Novelist*. London: Macmillan, 1981. A persuasive treatment of Hardy's acuteness in his characterizations. Sees Eustacia's identity in terms of her antipathy to the heath; argues that her death becomes inevitable when that identity is assimilated to the heath during the apocalyptic storm scene.

Woolf, Virginia. "The Novels of Thomas Hardy." In *The Common Reader,* Second Series. London: Hogarth Press, 1932. Regards Hardy's talent as a novelist as "unconscious"; sees Egdon Heath as central in *The Return* and argues that the novel is weakest in its treatment of social themes.

Wright, T. R. *Hardy and the Erotic*. London: Macmillan, 1989. A penetrating examination of the theme of desire in Hardy's fiction. Sees the complexity and sometimes even the confusion of Eustacia's characterization as a product of the tension between her function as an erotic object and her emergence as an erotic subject.

Zabel, Morton Dauwen. "Hardy in Defense of His Art: The Aesthetic of Incongruity." In *Hardy: A Collection of Critical Essays,* edited by Albert J. Guerard. Englewood Cliffs, N.J.: Prentice-Hall, 1963. Examines the importance of incongruity as an aesthetic principle in Hardy's novels.

Index

The Author

Brian Thomas has taught English at three Canadian universities—most recently, the University of Toronto, where he is currently director of the Writing Workshop at Victoria College. He is the author of *An Underground Fate: The Idiom of Romance in the Later Novels of Graham Greene* (1988).